DISCOVERY TRIPS IN
EUROPE

By the Editors of Sunset Books and Sunset Magazine

LANE PUBLISHING CO.
MENLO PARK, CALIFORNIA

Edited by **Cornelia Fogle**

Design: John Flack

Maps: Vernon Koski, Roberta Dillow

Special Consultant, Eastern Europe: Charles Mitchelmore

Cover. The rich textures of ancient stone glow warmly
in the walled village of St. Paul-de-Vence,
perched on its hilltop in the maritime Alps overlooking
the resorts of the French Riviera (see page 34).
Photograph by French Government Tourist Office.

Editor, Sunset Books: David E. Clark

Eighth Printing September 1978

Copyright © 1972, Lane Publishing Co.
Menlo Park, California 94025.
Second Edition. World rights reserved.

Burg Eltz, Mosel valley, Germany (see page 72).

CONTENTS

SPECIAL FEATURES

INTRODUCTION

More and more travelers are heading for Europe each year and finding that a first trip merely whets a person's travel appetite. Exploring Europe is now a possibility for many millions of people in this travel-conscious age; in increasing numbers, travelers return to Europe again and again to discover new regions and revisit favorite places.

Because sightseeing can be exhausting, the wise traveler mixes his travel to sample both city and country life. For it is in the European countryside that you gain a real appreciation of a country and its people.

A book of ideas

Discovery Trips in Europe is not a guidebook. It does not include detailed sightseeing information nor listings of hotels and restaurants. Other sources cover that material well.

It is a book filled with ideas, designed to add an extra dimension to your already exciting travel plans. Some of the trips have become reasonably well known, and rightly so. Other places have been visited by relatively few non-European travelers.

Some of these trips take less than a day and can be done on the spur of the moment; others need advance planning. First-time travelers will find trips easily worked into an itinerary, while others who have seen the well-known places will welcome new areas.

You'll discover Europe best outside the cities—wandering in walled towns little changed from medieval days, prowling through lively open-air markets with village housewives, buying wine for a picnic, cruising inland waterways through pastoral stillness, sharing a chocolate bar and a smile with strangers in a train compartment, sleeping in a castle fortress or an ancient inn.

Your visit will be richer and more satisfying if you follow your own hobbies and interests. Make history come alive as you seek out remnants of the past. Visit the homes where writers and artists lived and tour the countryside portrayed in their books and paintings. Collect new gardening ideas in Europe's outstanding parks and gardens. Try your favorite active sport in a new setting.

If possible, consider planning your trip in spring or fall, when you can enjoy Europe without the summer crowds. Off-season travelers experience some of Europe's most pleasant weather, and accommodations are easier to find—or to change on short notice.

Endless opportunities exist for each traveler, but only you can decide the experiences most important to you. This book will introduce you to some of the choices.

The joys of the countryside

For many experienced travelers, the real pleasure in Europe comes from traveling in the countryside. Here you experience the qualities making each region unique.

Cities are growing increasingly similar: hotels are larger and more impersonal; buildings are more modern; traffic is more hectic; people are more numerous. Each city's special qualities remain, but each year they are a little harder to discover.

Away from the cities, the pace of life slows. Cars are fewer, for in small towns many people walk or ride bicycles. People linger to talk with their neighbors and local shopkeepers or stop to pat a friendly dog.

There's a special charm in leisurely exploring. Off the main travel routes, country byways follow the contours of the land. You rediscover small pleasures: the patterns of cultivated fields, mountains cleanly etched against the sky, the various local ways that grape vines are staked or hay is stacked to dry in the sun.

You become aware of an amazing variety of physical regions within a country. Each region also has its own customs and traditions, and often its own local costumes and dialect, as well.

Outside the cities, sightseeing is less demanding, and you can let each day unfold with its events and adventures. Country hotels usually offer more charm and more personal attention than their big-city brothers. Often you can spend the night in a historic inn or a country castle.

A spirit of adventure

Travel should be fun, not a test of endurance. Cultural highlights are important, of course, but you'll remember the night you spent singing in an Irish pub far longer than the year that a city's cathedral was built.

Sharpen all your senses. The visitor who is content to "see Europe" misses much of the fun. Enjoy Europe's sights, but also taste its traditional dishes, listen to the vegetable sellers call out their wares, feel the cobblestones beneath your feet, smell the aroma of freshly-baked bread or the fragrance of flowers. If you are invited to participate in activities, do so with a smile.

In the placid waters of a Dutch canal, Kinderdijk's windmills cast a mirrorlike reflection.

Widen your interests to observe the people and their customs and try their foods and wines. If you explore a few places in depth, you'll feel like a traveler instead of a tourist.

Be willing to venture forth on your own, to experience the special pleasures reserved for travelers who take an occasional chance, try an unfamiliar food, or stop in an unknown town.

Many places are best explored on foot. Walk the cobbled alleyways where flowers cascade from stairways and balconies. Stride atop ancient ramparts encircling medieval towns. Linger near the harbor to watch fishermen auction the day's catch. You'll happen on colorful rural fairs and markets, pastoral countryside of unexpected beauty, and small towns where English-speaking visitors are a rarity.

When you explore on your own, getting briefly lost can be part of the fun, and it often opens the way to unanticipated discoveries—and lasting memories.

Discovering your own style

Since each person travels differently, part of the fun is discovering your own style of travel. For some people, travel planning is half the enjoyment. Their idea of a pleasant evening is to curl up with a map and guidebook. Others prefer loosely structured plans, taking each unscheduled day as it comes and meeting it on its own terms.

The person with limited time must decide on his most important travel goals; otherwise the days slip away too fast. Yet it is important to leave time for relaxed enjoyment of the passing scene and for unexpected activities.

Assembling your information

As you plan your trip, you'll find several sources of travel information. Your local library or bookstore probably stocks a selection of books on European countries.

When you decide on the countries you plan to visit, write to the individual foreign government tourist offices for information on specific regions of each country or special topics that interest you; the address of each tourist office will be found at the end of the appropriate chapter. These helpful representatives cannot help you plan your trip, but they can send a map and brochures on different parts of their country. Often they have information on camping, hotels, regional foods, shopping, children's activities, boat trips, sports, or similar subjects.

Well-traveled friends will probably pass on tips on places they particularly enjoyed. Your best suggestions will come from friends whose tastes and style of travel are similar to yours. Remember that each person has his special interests, and you can't do everything. When your time is limited, you must be selective and do the things *you* really want to do.

A qualified travel agent can handle many of the details for you. He can provide information on tours, arrange for plane and train tickets, make hotel reservations, and, if you wish, handle trip planning, including side trips and special events. Travel agencies do not usually charge for arranging transportation or for package tours, but they do charge for "custom" tour service. Be sure your agent understands clearly the type of accommodations and style of travel you desire.

In Europe, tourist offices are located in major cities and usually in medium-sized towns, as well.

When you venture off the beaten track, purchase a detailed map of the countryside. Though the maps in this book will assist you in locating points of interest, a regional map is helpful in finding secondary roads and small towns.

Getting around

Independent travel in Europe is not difficult. If you are traveling on your own, you will probably move around by a variety of means—plane, automobile, train, bus, boat, mountain railway, aerial cable car, on foot—possibly even by bicycle or on horseback. Varying your modes of transport adds spice to a trip.

On many of these trips, the most efficient way to see the country is by automobile. Rental cars are available in cities and major towns. If you prefer, your travel agent can reserve a car ahead for you. You'll find car rental agency offices in the downtown district and also in airport terminals. Many travelers prefer to begin their motoring excursion from the airport rather than start out in unfamiliar and often heavy city traffic.

If you have a choice of country where you plan to rent the car, compare rates *including taxes*. These vary considerably from country to country, and on an extended trip you can sometimes save a sizable amount by renting your car across the border. If you will be spending a major amount of time in one country, consider joining its national automobile club; membership provides many advantages.

Europe's efficient network of trains makes travel between cities and major towns a simple project. Many countries have special bargains for rail travelers; ask the foreign government tourist office for information on special rail travel tickets and excursions. Smaller towns are usually connected by local bus routes.

Within these pages you'll find mention of numerous boat trips, ranging from short city sightseeing excursions to cruises when the boat serves as your hotel.

Local customs vary

In your preliminary reading—and as you travel—you will discover local customs varying from your own familiar schedule. Each country has its traditional patterns. The happiest traveler is one who appreciates the differences and adjusts his own schedule and attitudes—treating variations as part of his travel experience.

Several basic guidebooks include information on holidays. You may decide to rearrange your schedule to attend a local celebration if you know about it in advance. Some government tourist offices issue periodic calendars of upcoming events.

Closing hours vary from country to country. In the British Isles, each town normally has early closing one afternoon each week, but the day varies by town. On the Continent, you'll sometimes find stores closed on Mondays. In a number of countries, shops and tourist attractions traditionally close for several hours at midday; shops may remain shuttered until late afternoon in hot countries, with activities resuming during the cooler hours of early evening.

Persons living in cities normally dine later than those living in the country. In general, the dinner hour is later in the warmer, southern countries than in northern Europe. If you have doubts, ask your hotel concierge about local customs.

Expect to pay an admission fee at most points of interest, although this may vary—in churches it often takes the form of an "offering box"; elsewhere you tip the guide. Observe what other travelers—particularly Europeans—are doing and take your cue from them.

One custom that surprises some first-time travelers is the added charge for carrying baggage in taxis in some cities, though this practice is not universal.

We acknowledge with appreciation

Many persons have helped in the preparation of this book, sharing their own travel discoveries and contributing suggestions and comments.

Special appreciation is due the many foreign government tourist officials who have provided supplementary information and photographs, helped us in our search for fresh travel ideas, and checked material before publication.

The European countryside offers a treasure chest of new and delightful experiences to the adventuresome traveler willing to venture off the main routes. Each traveler has his favorite routes, and you are encouraged to let us know other discoveries you would like to share.

Haying in Switzerland's Engadine valley above St. Moritz.

England's western tip

Pirates and smugglers cruised these waters

Travelers who visit Britain's southwestern tip must make a special effort, for it's not a stopping place along a route to another destination. Yet many visitors return again and again, drawn to this legendary sea-hewn land of King Arthur with its sturdy fishing towns and spectacular shoreline. In coastal villages you can listen to tales of smugglers and pirates; inland, you puzzle over strange stone markers left by a prehistoric civilization.

The time to visit is in May or June, when wildflowers bloom on the clifftops and along country lanes, or in autumn after the crowds are gone. During July and August, vacationing families swarm to coastal towns, which take on a commercial atmosphere.

Secure in their remote land, the men of Cornwall were barely touched by the Roman occupation or even by the Norman conquest. In the far west, the people had their own language, and the region developed its own atmosphere and character. Yet today it is not isolated; trains make numerous daily trips from London to West Country towns, and buses link additional towns and villages.

Dominating the region is the sea. You are seldom far from its sights, sounds, and smells. Along the northwestern coast, the cold blue Atlantic breaks along rugged headlands, while the south coast is lapped by the warmer, gentle waters of the English Channel. Since distances are short, you can spend the morning on one coast and the afternoon on the other.

The south coast

Every visitor has his favorite beaches, views, and villages. Perhaps you'll start from historic Plymouth, one of the chief ports during the reign of Elizabeth I. From its harbor Sir Francis Drake sailed forth in his *Golden Hind* to successfully circumnavigate the world and later to destroy the Spanish Armada. From the town's Barbican quay, the Pilgrims bade a last farewell in 1620 before setting forth on the *Mayflower* for an unknown land.

North of the city a toll bridge spans the River Tamar, linking Devon with Cornwall. The main roads are inland, but numerous byways stretch down to the sea.

Bays, creeks, and wooded estuaries indent Cornwall's sheltered south coast. Principal resorts are Looe, Fowey, St. Austell (natives pronounce them *Foy* and *Sozzle*), Falmouth, and Penzance. Even more delightful are the old villages and fishing ports, where narrow streets wind past color-washed houses to the water—towns such as Polperro (with a smugglers' museum), Mevagissey, Gorran Haven, Portholland, Portloe, Porthscatho, St. Mawes, Coverack, and Cadgwith. Some towns develop a self-conscious quaintness during the summer influx.

Inviting side roads and intriguingly-named villages easily seduce you into further exploring. Country lanes edged by hedgerows cut across cliff-top farmlands, and car ferries chug across river estuaries.

From Falmouth the route south to Lizard Point (a graveyard for ships) crosses Goonhilly Downs. Here you'll see not only prehistoric tumuli but also upturned saucers of a satellite receiving station.

Near Marazion, east of Penzance, the rocky island of St. Michael's Mount looms a half mile offshore. At low tide you can walk out by causeway; at other times you take a boat. You can visit the castle Mondays, Wednesdays, and Fridays.

Passengers and cars *cross the Fowey River by car ferry between the towns of Bodinnick (above) and Fowey.*

Colorful fishing towns dot the coastline of Devon and Cornwall. Only pedestrians and donkeys can negotiate the steep street in Clovelly (top left). Boats are beached by the receding tide at St. Ives (bottom). Freshly-caught fish are weighed and sold (center). Fishing boats moor in Polperro's sheltered harbor (right).

Cornwall's rugged western tip

From popular Penzance, you can make a loop around Cornwall's westernmost point. To the south lie the ports of Newlyn and Mousehole (locals call it *Muzzle*); then you head inland. Between Lamora and Treen, look for the famous "Merry Maidens" group of stones standing in a roadside field. Celtic legends claim these nine monoliths were maidens turned to stone for dancing on the Sabbath. In summer you can see plays in Porthcurno's well-known open-air theater.

Cornwall's headlands come to an abrupt stop at Land's End, where the sea crashes against the rocks. In early morning or late afternoon, you may have the point to yourself. On rare days you can see the Isles of Scilly.

These historic islands lie some 27 miles offshore, a transplanted bit of the Riviera. Accessible by boat or helicopter from Penzance, the islands have a mild climate where palm trees thrive and daffodils and narcissus bloom in midwinter. Hugh Town, on the island of St. Mary's, is the only real town; from here you travel to the "off islands" by inter-island launch. Because island life is simple, visitors should plan to wear old clothes.

From Land's End a splendid coastal road continues north to St. Ives, a colorful harbor town that has attracted a large artists' colony.

The Atlantic shore

Above St. Ives the main route heads inland, but you can follow minor roads and stay close to the sea. Dramatic granite cliffs rise above stretches of glorious sand on the Atlantic coast. Surfers challenge the long, rolling breakers at Perranporth, Newquay, and Bude. Attractive Padstow is a fishing harbor on the Camel River estuary.

Throughout Cornwall desolate chimneys and crumbling engine houses provide ghostly reminders of the Cornish tin mines, most now abandoned, which supplied the world from Biblical times to the mid-19th century.

Legends of King Arthur are woven into the region's Celtic fiber, but nowhere is the story more vivid than on the headlands of Tintagel. Beneath the crumbling walls of a 13th-century castle lie traces of an earlier stronghold, the legendary site of Arthur's castle. In the village, stop for a look at the old stone Post Office.

Boscastle typifies northern Cornwall, its small sheltered harbor enclosed by hills, a wooded valley inland. Many visitors will want to continue north to the Devonshire fishing town of Clovelly. You park your car above town and walk down a precipitous cobbled lane to the village; luggage goes down by donkey.

Across Bodmin Moor

If you're traveling south, you begin the ascent to wild and lonely Bodmin Moor southwest of Launceston. At Bolventor, in the center of the moor, is the isolated Jamaica Inn, a welcome sight today as it must have been to travelers of the past.

A short distance south you can drive past Dozmary Pool into which—Cornish legends claim—the sword Excalibur was thrown at King Arthur's command and caught by a white hand that drew it beneath the waters of the "lake."

Cozy villages of the Cotswolds

Inviting country roads lead to market towns and cozy hamlets

Dotted with honey-colored stone villages and cut by clear streams, the rolling green countryside of the Cotswold Hills is a very British part of England. Country roads and footpaths criss-cross the hills and meadows and valleys, climbing and dipping with the land. Many attractive small hamlets, built of the local golden-gray limestone, lie only short distances off the main roads, yet they are discovered by relatively few of the area's visitors who throng to the larger, well-known towns.

Less than a hundred miles northwest of London, the Cotswolds stretch approximately fifty miles from Chipping Campden in the north almost to Bath in the south.

You can make one of the towns your headquarters for touring the Cotswolds, and if you like, for Oxford and Stratford-on-Avon as well. Distances are short, and traffic is seldom heavy on the country roads. The nearest rail station is at Moreton-in-Marsh; local buses connect most of the main towns.

The best way to enjoy your visit is to settle into one of the cozy stone inns, buy a detailed map of the countryside, and set out by small car. With your map you're free to explore any temptingly-named village or inviting side road that strikes your fancy. If you ask in advance, perhaps the inn will pack a picnic lunch, or you can plan to be in one of the larger towns at mealtime.

The Cotswold villages

The northern Cotswolds are cut by Route A 429, which for part of its length follows an ancient Roman road known as Fosse Way. In Roman times the road cut diagonally across England more than 200 miles, from the Devonshire coast all the way to Lincoln. In later centuries monks, pilgrims, merchants, and highwaymen passed this way. Cirencester, Stow-on-the-Wold, and Moreton-in-the-Marsh are major Cotswold towns along the route.

In the 15th century, the Cotswolds were prolific producers of Britain's wool, and prosperous merchants endowed their towns and villages with splendid churches and fine houses. Native stone was used for building not only homes but also churches, farm buildings, and field walls.

Often the traveler is surprised by the charm of English villages, and nowhere more so than in the Cotswolds. They contain few of the well-known "sights," but during your visit you have the pleasure of becoming a villager yourself. There's no need to hurry as you stroll down the town's main street. You admire the inn's painted sign-board, buy stamps at the general store, watch ducks and swans on the pond, and admire the blooming roses and flowers cascading over weathered stone walls. You eat your meals in the local inn and in the evening join the villagers over a glass of ale.

To the Swells and Slaughters

Among the numerous routes to explore, none is more enjoyable than a side trip to Upper and Lower Swell and Upper and Lower Slaughter. This quartet of sleepy hamlets typifies all of the qualities that make Cotswold villages so attractive. You start your excursion in Stow-on-the-Wold, the highest village in the Cotswolds at

Children frolic on the grassy banks beside Upper Slaughter's meandering stream on a lazy day in late spring.

Villagers pause for a brief chat across the wall in Upper Slaughter (left). Stone houses line the curving river in Lower Slaughter, one of the prettiest of the Cotswold villages (top right). You feel like a giant when you stroll through the model village of Bourton-on-the-Water (bottom right).

760 feet, and finish in popular Bourton-on-the-Water.

Stow is set on a hilltop, with roads radiating out to different parts of the region. It has been a major market town for nearly 900 years, reaching the peak of its importance during the days when the wool industry flourished. A huge elm on one side of the market square shades the stocks where offenders were once punished and ridiculed; the old market cross is at the opposite end of the square. The pinnacled tower of Stow's parish church is a landmark for miles around.

You descend from Stow's hill along shaded route B 4077; the hamlet of Upper Swell lies about a mile northwest of Stow. Though tiny, the village is delightful. Just west of Upper Swell, turn south on a country road toward Lower Swell, then continue on to Upper Slaughter.

Park beneath the trees shading Upper Slaughter's small triangular village green, then wander up the path to the left toward the old cemetery and square-towered parish church. The churchyard overlooks a pleasing scene: rustic stone cottages and farm buildings face a shallow stream, crossed by a small, arched footbridge. You can picnic on a shaded, grassy knoll above the stream.

Beyond the village, turn left to Lower Slaughter, one of the prettiest of the Cotswold towns. Mellowed stone homes and cottages face the shallow river that flows through the center of Lower Slaughter, paralleling the roadway. Low stone and wooden footbridges span the water. An old mill, no longer in operation, is at one end of the village, the impressive parish church at the other.

Park your car at the far end of town, near the church.

From Lower Slaughter drive southeast to parklike Bourton-on-the-Water. The slow-moving River Windrush flows through the center of town, dividing the green park area and the buildings. Bourton is crowded on Sundays and holidays, but on other days you'll enjoy wandering its streets and lanes and visiting its shops. Behind the Old New Inn is a model of Bourton, its miniature buildings constructed of Cotswold stone.

Other Cotswold excursions

Here are some other routes in the Cotswold Hills that you might enjoy:

From Moreton-in-Marsh northwest to Chipping Campden via Bourton-on-the-Hill, Blockley, Paxford, Ebrington.

From Broadway southwest to Winchcombe via Stanton and Stanway.

From Stanway southeast to Bourton-on-the-Water along the River Windrush, via Temple Guiting, Guiting Power, and Naunton.

From Bourton-on-the-Water southeast to Burford via Little and Great Rissington, Great Barrington, Taynton.

From Northleach east to Burford along Sherborne Brook and the River Windrush, via Farmington, Sherborne, Windrush, and Little Barrington.

From Andoversford southeast to Bibury along the River Coln, via Withington, Chedworth, Fossebridge, and Coln St. Denis.

The "Inn Route" through England

Hospitality comes with a thatched roof and a tale of smugglers

You really haven't seen the English countryside if you haven't sampled a cross-section of the delightful country inns and pubs found in small towns and villages throughout England. The "local" is the village social center, at night filled with ruddy-faced villagers who drop in for conversation and their evening pint of bitter. Often a few rooms are available for overnight guests.

To find the pubs and inns, you must get off the motorways and the main "A" roads and pick the secondary "B" roads, which take you into the peaceful countryside of winding lanes and neat little villages. Thatched roof cottages or half-timbered buildings may lie around the next bend, or you may come upon an unusual country church or grass-rimmed lake.

In the countryside you'll find few restaurants; the pubs and inns are the places to eat, with plain but good country food. And for overnight guests, the inns are an experience: though they may be short on baths, they're loaded with atmosphere.

You could select one of the inns as your headquarters while you explore the Cotswolds, the Lake District, Devon and Cornwall, the Yorkshire moors, or one of England's other scenic regions, or while you spend a few days at fishing or golf or relaxing beside the sea.

Another plan is to sample several inns on a driving tour, perhaps following your own special interest or hobby — visiting outstanding gardens and ancestral homes, places of literary or historic interest, castles, or cathedrals. Many of the towns are accessible by local trains and buses. Even persons traveling by boat will find nearby inns and pubs, handy for a good meal or an overnight stop ashore.

Finding the inns

Nearly 700 selected inns — just a fraction of the approximately 50,000 inns in Britain — are listed and briefly described in *Stay at an Inn* ($1.25), a pocketsize booklet available from the British Travel Bookshop Ltd., 680 Fifth Avenue, New York, N.Y. 10019. Additional interesting places to stay or dine in the countryside are described in *Commended Country Hotels, Guest Houses, and Restaurants* ($1.50), available at the same address. London bookstores carry a variety of guides recommending good places for meals and overnight accommodations.

Brightly-painted signs *usually identify English country inns and pubs. Here are four of them: (from left) St. George & Dragon, Wargrave, Berkshire; Royal Oak, Wineham, Sussex; Cat & Custard Pot, Shelton, Bedfordshire; Adam & Eve Inn, Buckland-in-the-Moor, Devon.*

Relaxed pace gives you time to enjoy the small pleasures. Guests take refreshment in the garden at Cott Inn, Dartington, Devon; watch a game of darts at Lord Crewe Arms, Blanchland, Northumberland; chat in the cobblestone courtyard of the Crown & Thistle, Abingdon, Berkshire; quench their thirst at the Bull Inn, Long Melford, Suffolk.

Persons who will be motoring in England and Scotland may wish to consider purchasing membership in the Royal Automobile Club (RAC) or the Automobile Association (AA). Both organizations offer a variety of services for members, and each publishes a book listing recommended hotels and restaurants.

As you travel on country roads and through small towns, you'll find the inns and pubs easy to spot. Many carry signs portraying such colorful names as Shoulder of Mutton, Star and Eagle, Seven Sisters, Rose Revived, Plume of Feathers, and Smugglers' Haunt.

No two inns are alike. In age, they range from medieval to modern. Some proudly recall their ties to such historic figures as Oliver Cromwell or Sir Francis Drake; others mark associations with the well-known literary names of Charles Dickens and John Keats. Many of the inns were once hideouts for smugglers or highwaymen; others sheltered the clergy in bygone days. Some are Tudor inns with oak-beamed ceilings or old coaching inns with cobbled courtyards. Others have thatched roofs or were built with stones from Hadrian's Wall. But all offer friendly hospitality at reasonable prices.

What you can expect

However different they may appear, most inns do have some things in common. The majority are relatively small, usually containing from three to twenty rooms (although some inns are larger). Most have a friendly polished-copper-and-brass pub. The reception desk is often tucked away in a closet, and you'll sign the register on the hall table. You won't find an elevator, and you may have to carry your own suitcase up the stairs. You will probably have to do without a private bath, sharing the one down the hall. A happy note: the cost of your room includes a substantial English breakfast, and the inn usually serves lunch and dinner as well.

While these accommodations will not suit every traveler, inns do have an undeniable charm. The annoyance of a creaking floor will be offset by the cheery sounds of birds chirping in the rose garden.

In popular areas the inns fill quickly, so you may want to telephone ahead to the next place to book your room. Non-guests who wish to sample the hospitality may book a table in the dining room for lunch or dinner, if space permits.

At the time you register, you can order early morning tea in your room and your favorite English newspaper, that you'll find beside your breakfast plate next morning.

The atmosphere is quiet and reserved, yet friendly. Before and after dinner, guests gather in the lounge, where a well-behaved dog may eye them from beside his mistress's feet. On Sundays the inns may offer "high tea," a substantial cold repast served in late afternoon in lieu of hot lunch and dinner.

Exploring along Hadrian's Wall

In the lonely north, you follow the paths of the Roman legions

Far to the north of England, the Roman Wall snakes across the rolling green hills of Northumberland and Cumberland. The wild and lonely countryside, often veiled by low-hanging mist and chilled by a stiff northwest wind, still retains the mood of the frontier. Yet the main Roman settlements are never far from Route B 6318, which parallels the wall for most of its way.

Built following a visit to Britain by Emperor Hadrian in 122 A.D., the wall extended 73 miles (80 Roman miles) across the narrow neck of England. It begins at Bowness, west of Carlisle on Solway Firth, and crosses to Wallsend, east of Newcastle near the mouth of the Tyne River. The wall was the northernmost defense line of the Roman Empire, a barrier against the savage Highlanders whom the Romans could not tame. Only sections of the wall now remain.

Hexham makes a good base for travelers, or you may decide to establish headquarters in one of the small local inns; you'll find them in Blanchland, Corbridge, Chollerford, Haltwhistle, and Wall. In a day you can easily see three of the major excavations and their museums, climaxing your visit with a long, invigorating walk atop the wall itself.

Along the Roman frontier

From Hexham, travel east on Route A 69 to Corbridge, then northwest a half mile to the site of Corbridge Roman Station. Located at the crossing of two major Roman roads, Corbridge became an important supply depot and military town during the advance into Scotland.

Numerous secondary roads head northwest toward Chollerford. Chesters Fort is along Route B 6318 about five miles north of Hexham, on the bank of the North Tyne River. At one time the fort garrisoned a cavalry regiment of 500. The cavalry was the elite of the Roman army, and accommodations here included a Roman bathhouse near the river. Sheep graze freely in the lush fields, so watch your step.

Perhaps the most striking setting belongs to Housesteads Fort, 8½ miles west of Chollerford. Here the wall follows a ridge, steep on the north and sloping gently to the south. The Roman fort lies along the crest, overlooking Knag Burn Valley. Excavations are still going on, but you can easily discern the layout of the buildings. If you look closely, you can see ruts made in the sills of the East Gate by cart wheels and scars on the water tank where soldiers sharpened their swords.

A well-preserved section of the wall lies to the west of Housesteads Fort. Go up the steps, climb over the stile, and make your way along the rocky dirt rim toward Cuddy's Crags and the milecastle. From atop the wall, you look north across the deep valley to dark green Northumbrian forests; in the mist and biting wind, you may feel a bit of the loneliness and isolation of the Roman soldiers who once trod this same path.

Visitors who wish to learn more of the Roman era in Britain can find numerous descriptive and historical booklets available. Two special Ordnance Survey maps have been published: a large-scale map of *Hadrian's Wall* and one of *Roman Britain*.

Walkers head west from Housesteads atop the Roman Wall. This section of the wall is preserved by the National Trust.

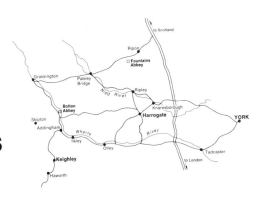

Sampling the Yorkshire dales

Visit gutted medieval abbeys and the wild Brontë country

Rock-strewn path *crosses the lonely Haworth Moor to the Brontë waterfall. Dry rock walls ascend far hillsides.*

Not for every traveler is the solitude of Yorkshire's moors and dales, but those who seek out its hidden pleasures will be well rewarded. From high in the Pennine range, rivers flow and tumble through the green hills, down valleys known as the Yorkshire dales. Ruins of ancient abbeys, looted and burned in the 16th century by troops of Henry VIII, still stand as reminders of the awesome wealth and power of the medieval church. And in the moorland village of Haworth, memories linger of the Brontë sisters, whose novels captured the wild beauty of the bleak Yorkshire countryside.

Ilkley, Skipton, and Harrogate are the usual centers for touring the Yorkshire dales. If you are using local transportation, take the train to Ilkley, then use buses to reach Haworth or to continue up Wharfedale.

You can sample the Yorkshire dales—a national park—on a loop trip following the Wharfe River to Grassington, returning by a different route.

The ruins of Bolton Abbey, overlooking the Wharfe in a green and lovely setting, have fascinated painters and provide a pleasant outing for ruddy-cheeked English families. Built in 1151, the monastery once sheltered 200 people before it was surrendered to the king's forces. Follow the path upriver into Bolton Woods, through some of the country's loveliest river scenery. A mile above the abbey, the Wharfe funnels into a narrow chasm of rushing white water, called The Strid.

Beyond Bolton Woods the road climbs into the grassy dales, criss-crossed by dry stone walls and public paths. Sheep and cattle graze in solitude. Only an occasional abandoned stone building marks its former habitation.

From Pateley Bridge you can return to York through Nidderdale, or you can head northeast toward Ripon, with a stop at the ruins of Fountains Abbey, another 12th-century monastery sacked by the king's troops during the dissolution of the monasteries in 1539-40.

Brontë country

Detour south from Addingham to the small moorland village of Haworth, rich in memories of the Brontë sisters, the three daughters of the local parson who brought literary recognition to the village.

The harsh reality of the Industrial Revolution confronts you at Keighley, its woolen mills rising starkly against the sky with tired, smoke-blackened houses clustering nearby. Follow highway signs toward Halifax until you come to the Haworth turnoff.

Stone blocks, set like steps to keep horses' hoofs from slipping, still pave Haworth's steep main street. In the simple stone parsonage facing the grim churchyard, the girls and their brother Branwell began writing as a childish game during long winters. Later the lonely moorlands they knew so well became the setting for their best novels—Charlotte's *Jane Eyre*, Emily's *Wuthering Heights*, Anne's *The Tenant of Wildfell Hall*. The parsonage has been restored to appear much like the Brontës knew it. An adjoining museum contains handwritten manuscripts, letters, and first editions.

If the day is pleasant, button your coat against the winds and follow the footpath across the moors to the Brontë waterfall (about 1¼ miles from the paved road), where a small creek tumbles down the valley. You may have the path to yourself, with only sheep for company.

East Anglia's charming villages

Seek out the scenic back roads in Essex and Suffolk

English villages provide sudden delights for the traveler who strikes off the main routes and risks getting lost on country byways. Few regions have preserved as well as East Anglia the appearance and spirit of medieval times. Many a village retains its rich legacy of timbered houses and ancient buildings, oak-paneled inns and solid churches.

When you venture onto East Anglia's back roads, you'll discover such delightful hamlets as Thaxted on its hilltop; Kersey, where a shallow stream crosses the main road; half-timbered Lavenham; Cavendish, with its thatched roofs; and the pargetted houses of Clare.

The wool boom of the 14th, 15th, and 16th centuries heaped prosperity on the towns and villages of Essex and Suffolk, as it did elsewhere in England. Wealthy merchants and traders spent their money freely on fine houses and great parish churches. In each town the church is a focal point, its tower or spire rising prominently above the buildings and peaceful countryside.

Establish yourself in the local inn, then wander into the streets to see what the town offers you. Perhaps you'll see a thatcher renewing the reed roof on a cottage, or a game of skittles (similar to bowling) or cricket on the village green. Time seems to slow down as you meander along, absorbing the village's character.

Essex towns and villages

In northern Essex you drive through rural countryside, acres of farmlands and cornfields with occasional patches of woods. Saffron Walden is an interesting old town, a haphazard jumble of ancient inns and modern shopping center, half-timbered houses and market stalls overflowing with farm produce. A 17th-century Jacobean mansion, Audley End House, is open from April to October (closed Mondays).

Thaxted is perhaps the most charming of the Essex villages. Many timbered and plastered houses line its winding cobblestone streets, and the town has a distinctive guildhall. High above town stands the fine limestone church, adorned with carved gargoyles, animals, and birds, a permanent reminder of the age when the town was a wealthy wool center.

A country road leads east to the villages of Little Bardfield and Great Bardfield, then on to photogenic Finchingfield. Immaculately-preserved houses and a curving street center upon a large green that slopes down to a pond. Rising against the skyline is the town's 11th-century church.

A few miles beyond is Sible Hedingham, where you meet the Colne River wending its lazy way to the sea. The high-set Norman keep of Hedingham Castle is visible long before you reach it; from the 12th-century castle you have fine views over the countryside.

You follow the scenic river road down the valley, crossing the Colne several times and passing through several pleasant villages. At Earls Colne detour south to Coggeshall, once a main weaving center but now a village. The big attraction is Paycocke's, a richly ornamented merchant's house built about 1500, but the town also has a remarkable collection of half-timbered Tudor houses. You'll also see a fine display of the traditional

Finchingfield's parish church dominates the skyline. Villagers pause on the green, and a swan glides across the pond.

Curving street in Kersey is crossed by a shallow, shaded stream (left). Trim houses and a massive 15th-century church border Long Melford's village green (top). Workman trims the thatch on a cottage roof in East Anglia (bottom center). Quaint gabled row cottages and a windmill are part of Thaxted's quiet charm (bottom right).

East Anglian craft of pargetting, in which outside walls are decorated with ornamental plaster moulds.

Along the Stour

The meandering Stour River marks the boundary between the counties of Essex, south of the river, and Suffolk, to the north. Inviting high-hedged lanes branch off the main road, and you'll enjoy white and strawberry-washed plaster and timber cottages.

Sudbury, a sturdy country market town, was the birthplace of painter Thomas Gainsborough; his birthplace is now a Gainsborough museum.

The lush pastoral countryside of river, woods, and meadows near the mouth of the Stour is known as the Constable country, named after landscape artist John Constable. Born in East Bergholt, he roamed this untroubled valley during the years the American colonists were fighting for independence. Near Dedham is Flatford Mill, the subject of one of his best-known works, remaining much the same as it was in Constable's day.

Byways in sleepy Suffolk

Some of East Anglia's most delightful villages and towns are sprinkled along the upper Stour and its tributary streams. In quiet Suffolk, often you can drive for miles without coming upon another car.

In Hadleigh you'll see town houses and mansions from Tudor, Elizabethan, and Jacobean periods, as well as smaller houses and cottages in the half-timbered style.

Cottages line Kersey's attractive main street; its church sits high above on a hill. You'll have the novel experience of fording a shallow, tree-shaded stream flowing across the road. The wool town of Kersey gave its name to a coarse cloth, while nearby Lindsey provided its name for linsey-woolsey, a fabric that clothed many American colonials.

Lavenham's wool-trading forebears built a magnificent perpendicular-style church, but this picture-postcard Suffolk town is even better known for its wealth of black-and-white timber-framed cottages and venerable inns, whose top stories often bulge over the lower ones.

You'll find another fine church in Long Melford, where buildings line two miles of the town's main street. Here, also, are two impressive mansions, Kentwell Hall, with its moat, and Melford Hall.

A few miles west along the upper Stour are the attractive riverside villages of Cavendish and Clare. Cavendish has a wide green and many thatched cottages, and Clare contains numerous delightful old houses with East Anglian pargetting.

If you're ready for a change of pace, head north to Newmarket, a horse-crazy town for over 250 years. On race days it is swamped by lively, enthusiastic crowds of horse-lovers; at other times, Newmarket is a staid, open-air country town strung along a wide main street. Most of the country's valuable racing thoroughbreds are trained here. Often you'll see lithe little jockeys and stableboys around the rambling stables, and elegant racehorses and their riders enjoying a practice trot on the rolling grasslands encircling the town.

By boat through Britain

Cruise along England's idyllic canals and rivers

Seeing England by boat provides a special pleasure—the relaxation of a cruise combined with ever-changing scenery, interesting towns and villages to visit, and opportunities for meeting the friendly river and canal folk.

From the deck of a cabin cruiser, you see the busy Thames-side towns glide past as you cruise under arching canal bridges and pass through well-kept river locks, each with its own tidy garden.

Then you pass from the broad waterways to the more secluded canals, where by narrow canal boat you probe the undiscovered life of the quiet countryside, far from roads and traffic. You may meet some of the long "narrow-boats" (painted with the traditional decorations of "roses and castles") which have plied the canals for

150 years. You tie up along the towpath for refreshments at boatmen's inns.

The invigorating coastal air of the Norfolk Broads can be yours on a sailing, cruising, or houseboating holiday. Here you cruise through wide tidal estuaries, bounded by grassy slopes and fine trees, and up tiny estuaries, where ducks and coots and moorhens dart in and out among the reeds, and windmills appear against the skyline.

Your holiday afloat

Boats and excursions are available to suit a wide variety of requirements and tastes. Accommodation aboard the boats is comfortable. You can either skipper your own boat or hire someone to do it for you. No previous experience is necessary; the boatyard operator will give you instructions before you set out.

You'll find motor cruisers, narrow canal boats, houseboats, and sailing yachts available for rent. Most boats have two to six berths, although larger ones will accommodate up to 12 people. Energetic boaters can explore freely in a rented camping punt or canoe.

If you prefer, you can join a week's cruise on the River Thames or the canals of the Midlands. Your route will be planned and an experienced crew will handle the navigation and cooking. If time is limited, perhaps a two-day "mini cruise" along the Thames will fit into your schedule.

Once you decide that a boating holiday in England has intriguing possibilities, write to the British Tourist Authority for the booklet *Holidays on Inland Waterways*. This contains information on the navigable waterways and a listing of boat hire firms and cruise operators. Many of the firms participate in a central information and booking agency—Skipper Holidays Afloat, 210 California Avenue, Palo Alto, Calif. 94306. Write to them for *A Lazy Man's Guide to Holidays Afloat* ($1.50).

Canal and river cruises

Several firms operate cruises for passengers who prefer to enjoy the sights without worrying about the details.

*At **Sonning** on the Thames River (above Henley), boats large and small await their turn to pass through the river lock.*

Splendid meandering is a treat along country waterways, here on the Thames near Clifton Hampden (left). Many narrow-boats are painted in traditional designs (center). Sailors rendezvous in the Norfolk Broads (right).

Cruisers or converted narrow-boats provide accommodations in single and double cabins with hot and cold running water; showers and toilets are usually down the hall. During the day or evening, travelers can relax in the lounge. Most boats have a small licensed bar; some have a shipboard library. Meals are served family style in the dining area. Along the way you can enjoy peaceful walks, visit some friendly country pubs, and explore market towns near the waterways.

Several firms operate regular canal cruises using traditional narrow-boats converted into self-contained floating hotels. The boats usually travel in pairs along the canals and rivers; the motorboat tows an unpowered "butty." Each pair of boats carries 8 to 12 passengers. Cost varies from about $110 to $150 per person per week for accommodations and meals.

A modern 70-foot cruiser transports 10 passengers on 3 or 6-day cruises through the open landscape of the Norfolk Broads.

On the River Thames you can make 3 or 6-day cruises from Reading on a 12-passenger boat operated by River Barge Holidays Ltd., 7 Walton Well Road, Oxford.

If time is limited but you'd still like to sample river life, a 2-day Thames Valley "mini-cruise" operates between Windsor and Oxford from mid-July to mid-August. You travel from London to Windsor by rail and return from Oxford the same way. During the days, you cruise upriver on an excursion steamer. Light refreshments are served on board, and you dock for meals and overnight accommodations ashore. Cruise operator is Salter Brothers Ltd., Folly Bridge, Oxford.

From April through September, day boat trips from London cruise down the Thames to the Tower of London and Greenwich. Or try the upriver cruise to Kew, Richmond, Kingston, and Hampton Court.

For a unique view of London, take a trip in a traditionally painted narrow-boat along the Regent's Canal from Little Venice (Paddington) through Regent's Park and the London Zoo to the Camden Town Locks. During the summer, "water bus" service operates between Paddington's Little Venice and the London Zoo to Regent's Park.

A network of waterways

The canal age began in the mid-18th century when an interlacing network of inland waterways was built for transporting freight throughout the country. But the railways, and later the roads, moved the vast cargoes faster, and today little commercial traffic operates on the canals and rivers that meander through the quiet countryside. Diesel motors have replaced the horses that once pulled the canal boats.

Most of the canals pass through meadows and woodland and sleepy hamlets, rather than large towns. Soon the fast pace of shore life is replaced by a sense of tranquillity and contentment. By slow boat you cruise along a channel so narrow you feel you're floating through the meadow. Grazing cows may turn to watch you pass by. You'll see sheep in the fields, swans and moorhens along the bank, and you may even hear a cuckoo.

Negotiating locks can add to the fun; a lock-keeper operates each of the Thames locks, but on the canals you work them yourself (the hiring firm will show you how). Passengers can walk along the tow paths beside the canals. Each evening you moor near a village, where you vary on-board cooking with dinner in the local inn.

Along the Grand Union Canal in rural Northamptonshire, you'll come to the canal-side village of Stoke Bruerne, interesting for its hump-back bridge, boatmen's inn, and lock. Here you'll find the Waterways Museum (open March to October), with fascinating exhibits which bring to life 200 years of inland waterway history.

Sailors will head for the Norfolk Broads, where sailing boats and motor cruisers crowd the waters in peak season. The Broads are a mass of lakes and "wides" connected by numerous rivers, which wind slowly through flat green countryside toward the sea. Birds nest along the waterways, and you'll see an occasional windmill on the horizon.

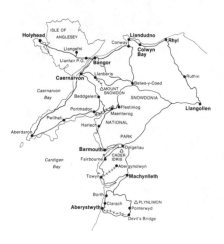

Exploring northern Wales

You'll find a warm welcome and an uncomplicated holiday

What does a visitor remember most about Wales? Probably the wild and wonderful beauty of the Welsh hills and the warmth of the people.

Welshmen love their country with a fierce devotion. Pushed into the western mountains during ancient battles with the Saxons, they defended their land passionately against all invaders, retreating to impregnable mountain strongholds. Still guarding the green valleys are the crumbling towers of battle-scarred fortresses like Harlech, Conway, and Caernarvon, built in the 13th century by English invaders.

Major routes intersect in the Caernarvonshire town of Beddgelert. You'll find British highways well marked.

In many ways, Wales remains a remote country within a country. Although part of Britain, it has retained its unique identity, clinging to an ancient Celtic language (whose literature goes back 1,400 years) and to many of its traditions. Although place names with their complicated spellings may puzzle you, you'll be relieved to know that everyone speaks English—with a charming lilt. Since there are few large towns, the best way to tour Wales is by car.

The northern coast

Many visitors entering North Wales from England head for Llangollen, where each July singers and dancers in national dress, representing over 30 countries, compete in the International Musical Eisteddfod.

Medieval buildings, spanning several centuries, crowd Ruthin's small square. In Ruthin Castle, now a hotel, you can enjoy a three-hour Elizabethan-style banquet, complete with Welsh music and song.

The seaside towns of Rhyl, Colwyn Bay, and Llandudno offer the usual diversions of English coastal resorts. Nearby is Conway, the town walls and 21 towers of its well-preserved castle rising grandly above the river.

For quiet holidays

Near Bangor you can stop at Penrhyn Castle, a National Trust parkland and museum with historic railway vehicles and a large doll collection.

Across Menai Strait from Bangor is the Isle of Anglesey, joined to the mainland by bridge, rail, and ferry. The island is a favorite retreat of vacationers seeking an informal, inexpensive holiday. On nearly every visitor's route is the unpretentious village known as Llanfair P.G., a mercifully shortened form of its full name:

Llanfairpwllgwyngyllgogerychwyrndrobwll-
llantysyliogogogoch.

Though it's a descriptive name, to anyone other than a Welshman it's almost impossible to pronounce. It means "St. Mary's (Church) by the white aspen over the

Scenic Pass of Aberglaslyn (left) is reached by the Beddgelert-Portmadoc road. North Wales resort of Llandudno stretches along the sea front (top). The narrow-gauge Talyllyn Railroad has carried passengers for over a hundred years (bottom center). Massive walls of Harlech Castle have withstood sieges (bottom right).

whirlpool and St. Tysilio's (Church) by the red cave." You can see the name over the local garage; the railway signpost is in the railway section of Penrhyn Castle Museum. The main road continues across Anglesey to Holyhead, terminus of the ferry from Ireland.

One of Wales' main attractions is historic Caernarvon Castle, scene of the 1969 investiture of Prince Charles as Prince of Wales.

Thrusting westward into the Irish Sea is Lleyn Peninsula, the "land's end" of North Wales. Its gorse-covered slopes and breezy headlands seem a world apart, and you'll delight in the old-world atmosphere of small farms and old villages. The main holiday centers are along the southern coast—Aberdaron, Abersoch, Pwllheli, and Criccieth.

The realm of Snowdonia

The high and rugged mountains of Snowdonia, once a natural fortress against invaders, are today a favorite destination of outdoorsmen. You may see climbers near the Llanberis Pass.

You can tour parts of Snowdonia National Park by car or mountain railway, picnic under the trees, or explore on foot. Nature trails leave from Beddgelert, Betws-y-Coed, Capel Curig, Maentwrog, and Pen-y-Gwryd.

Riding miniature trains

Young and old will enjoy a trip on one or more of the five small passenger railways along this route. Trains operate during the tourist season, from spring into fall. Check locally for schedules and fares.

The Snowdon Mountain Railway, Britain's only rack-and-pinion railway (built in 1896) takes passengers from Llanberis on a 7-mile round trip up Snowdon peak.

From Portmadoc, at the mouth of the Glaslyn River, the Festiniog Narrow Gauge Railway (built in 1836) travels into the hills above the Vale of Ffestiniog.

At Fairbourne, the miniature Fairbourne Railway makes a short, 1½-mile trip to Penrhyn Point.

Another century-old narrow-gauge steam train is the Talyllyn Railway, traveling from the coastal town of Towyn inland to Abergynolwyn.

From the resort of Aberystwyth, British Rail operates the narrow gauge Vale of Rheidol Railway, up the wooded Rheidol valley to Devil's Bridge.

Along Cardigan Bay

Continuing south, you'll soon reach the ruins of Harlech Castle, another in the ring of fortresses built in the 13th century by the invading English troops.

Barmouth faces the Mawddach estuary; you can ferry across toward Fairbourne. The scenic Cader Idris range bulges toward the sea near Towyn, terminus of the Talyllyn Railway. Aberystwyth is the main town and resort on the Cardigan shore; from here you can drive or take the small train up one of Wales' loveliest valleys, the wooded Vale of Rheidol.

If you are returning north, you can view an exhibit of Welsh crafts and textiles at Machynlleth.

ADDING ZEST TO CITY EXPLORATIONS

Most travelers fall into familiar sightseeing patterns when they visit Europe's major cities. Each capital has its recognized attractions, and it's all too easy to confine sightseeing to a guidebook's suggestions or a tour director's recommendations.

But take an afternoon off and venture forth to make your own city discoveries. Your own hobbies and interests will often suggest ideas.

Go window shopping. On a day when you have no special purchases planned, take an hour or two and study the displays in shop windows. Particularly off the main shopping thoroughfares, you'll find European stores have their own special ways of displaying foods and merchandise. In a department store, wander through a section which especially appeals to you — for example, housewares or hardware, fabrics or the delicatessen. Along with many familiar items, you'll often find some new and useful ones.

Adopt "your" sidewalk cafe. Pick out a convenient cafe, one near your hotel, perhaps, where you can visit daily at the same hour, both for refreshment and to participate in one of Europe's favorite sports: "people watching." Late afternoon is a pleasant time, when you can relax after the day's activities before readying yourself for dinner.

Pursue your favorite hobby. If you're a stamp collector, visit a stamp market (there's a good one in Paris). Good cooks can look for a new kitchen gadget or food product to try. Gardeners can go on an idea-collecting walk in city parks and gardens.

Seek out an offbeat museum. Persons who associate museums only with art are in for a surprise. You can visit maritime and railway displays, homes of famous people, collections of all kinds, and museums on subjects as varied as bullfighting (Madrid), breweries (Dublin, Brussels, and other cities), skiing (Oslo), and royal coaches (Lisbon and Munich).

Try a new food idea. Sample an unfamiliar food or one you'd normally not try — raw herring and onions in Amsterdam, for example, or smoked eel *smörrebröd* in Copenhagen. You might find that you like it. Sidewalk stalls dispense some interesting local favorites.

View the city from the water. Most cities are built on a coast or major inland waterway. Usually you'll find that a sightseeing cruise — on harbor, lake, river, or canals — provides new views and perspectives.

Wander in an open-air market. Europe's traditional outdoor markets are a delight (see page 38). You can select the type most interesting to you. Nearly every large city offers at least one outdoor market.

Visit the park. Europe's city parks are a delight, with gardens, walking paths, and diversions for the entire family. Saturday and Sunday afternoons are the family days in the parks. You can ride a ferris wheel, rent a boat for a row on the lake, watch a Punch and Judy show, relax in an outdoor cafe, listen to a band concert, or just sit on a bench and enjoy the life flowing by.

Make a new friend. Your friends at home, a professional organization, or a service club can often provide names of persons living abroad with whom you may enjoy getting acquainted. Government tourist information offices can provide information on hospitality programs, where you meet a local person or family with interests similar to yours.

Discover a city's human side when you observe and meet the people; (left to right) have lunch in a London pub, adopt a sidewalk cafe in Paris, spend Sunday afternoon in the park — here, in Vienna's Prater.

Into the Scottish Highlands

Explore heather-covered hills and watch pipers parade

North of Edinburgh lie placid green glens, silvery lochs, and the wild heather-covered moors of the Scottish Highlands. Many Scots enjoy active holidays in fishing, golfing, hill-walking, pony-trekking, and mountaineering, and you can join them. In late summer, attend a gathering of Highland clans.

From the Scottish capital you cross the wide Firth of Forth, headed north toward Perth. Sir Walter Scott called Perthshire "the fairest portion of the Northern Kingdom," and truly it has some of Scotland's finest scenery. Surrounded by rich farmland, the pleasant market town of Perth sits astride the River Tay. To the north, you climb into ever-higher and wilder heather-splotched hills. Shakespeare's tragedy, *Macbeth*, was set in this lonely countryside.

In Dunkeld you can visit the 17th-century "Little Houses," restored by the National Trust. In summer, Pitlochry presents plays in its "Theatre in the Hills." You continue on the Great North Road into the heart of the Highlands, where heather grows down to the roadside. Sometimes you'll see a herd of deer grazing on a hilltop, and in the stillness you may hear the sound of a grouse or a distant curlew. At Kingussie you can stop at the Highland Folk Museum.

Fort William and Inverness are gateway towns to the wild and majestic scenery of the northwest. The highway linking them follows the Caledonian Canal. As you pass Loch Ness, keep a sharp eye out for a glimpse of "Nessie," the monster reputed to live in its dark waters.

The holiday center of Aviemore offers fishing in the River Spey, chairlift rides up the Cairngorm Mountains (where there's fine skiing in winter), and a vast nature reserve and forest park to explore. The Highlands visitor center in Carrbridge displays Highland crafts and exhibits. East from Carrbridge toward Grantown-on-Spey, the route is spotted with whisky distilleries.

The busy port of Aberdeen is the center for visitors enjoying scenic Deeside, the valley west of the city. The road closely parallels the twisting River Dee all the way to Braemar, site of a great Highland gathering each September. On the way you come to Balmoral, the castle where the British royal family vacations in late summer. When they are not in residence, visitors can walk around the castle grounds.

Golfers will want to visit old St. Andrews; here the sport has been played for over 500 years. Rent clubs, if you like, and play the historic course (see page 25).

Gatherings of the Highland clans

From July to September, tartan-clad men and lassies of Scotland's clans congregate in a holiday mood at a number of Highland gatherings. To the high-pitched skirl of bagpipes and the roll of drums, muscled giants compete in arduous feats of strength—tossing the caber, putting the shot, throwing the long-handled hammer. Marching bands in black-feather bonnets parade, their kilts and sporrans swinging with each step. Dancers display nimble footwork in a brisk reel or lively Highland fling.

The most famous gathering is at Braemar, attended by the Queen and members of the royal family, but other Highland gatherings are held throughout the north and west of Scotland. For information or a schedule, stop in at the Scottish Tourist Board office in Edinburgh.

Balmoral Castle, *Highland retreat of Britain's royal family, stands amid forested hills along Scotland's River Dee.*

A walk in the Pentland Hills

Shoulder your knapsack for a day in the hills near Edinburgh

A walk through the pasture-moorland of Scotland's Pentland Hills will give you a chance to stretch your legs and to find out just why the Scotsman loves his hills.

The charm of Robert Louis Stevenson's treasured "hills of home" lies in their many slopes and glens, in the splatterings of "stone glint" (sunlight on wet rocks), and in the luminous light which seems to radiate from rocks, plants, and streams. Clouds constantly shift and reform with the wind; a hillside which appears all red earth and yellow furze in the sunlight changes to patterns of green and blue and violet when a cloud passes under the sun.

You climb the windswept hills like stairs, threading your way over grass and rocks, among sheep and patches of gorse and heather. Daisies, buttercups, bluebells, and yellow coltsfoot brush your ankles. Bracken uncurls its light green fronds in spring and gleams bright gold in autumn. Only an occasional bird song or the bark of a shepherd's dog breaks the silence.

The Pentland range begins three miles south of Edinburgh and extends 16 miles to the southwest, with an average width of 4½ miles. Few peaks are over 1,500 feet high. If you use the bus and streetcar services that almost encircle the hills—but don't penetrate them—you can take walks of any length from 2 to 20 miles.

Getting ready

Before you start out, be sure you have a pedestrian's map of the Pentland Hills and Edinburgh District, available in Edinburgh bookstores.

Pack a shoulder knapsack with sandwiches, sweet biscuits (cookies), fruit, chocolate bars, and a vacuum bottle filled with hot ginger. Unless it's your first day in Scotland, you won't need to be reminded to bring a raincoat. High rubber-soled shoes or short boots are best for footwear, for the ground is boggy in places.

If you take the trails shown above, you'll begin your all-day trek at St. Andrews Square in Edinburgh's New Town, where you take the "S.M.T." bus for Balerno.

On the trail

Leave the bus at Balerno, shoulder your knapsack, and head upward, following the road to the left of the church and the inn. When the road forks, keep right past Upper Dean Park and over Threipmuir Reservoir. At the end of the road, turn left past dark gray Bavelaw Castle, almost hidden in trees. You'll find a fence to climb. Guideposts mark the path before you climb over a wooden stile.

Look at your map and you'll see there are five hills between you and Edinburgh. Climb the first three on your route; at Harbour Hill you have a choice.

The shorter route descends on your right to Glencorse Reservoir and will lead you to the inn at Flotterstone just about teatime. Buses for Edinburgh stop hourly.

If you decide on the longer hilltop route (for a total trek of about 14 miles), you'll be rewarded with one of Scotland's finest views from the top of Allermuir Hill.

Below and to the left of Swanston, Stevenson's old home is still visible among the trees. You'll leave the hills to walk over grass-covered boggy ground around Swanston Burn, climb over a fence, and take the double-decked No. 11 bus back to Princes Street.

Footpaths *wind through green pastureland and across the windswept moorlands of Scotland's Pentland Hills.*

IN BRITAIN: special interests

LONDON'S VILLAGES ● Several of the once-rural villages absorbed during London's outward spread still stubbornly retain much of their village character. *Hampstead* is only a few minutes from Piccadilly Circus by underground railway, yet the city seems distant as you stroll old-world streets and stride over the open expanse of Hampstead Heath. On the other side of the heath is *Highgate*, where you admire gracious 18th-century houses and take refreshment at an inn beneath cherry trees.

Kew, with its Royal Botanic Garden, has a village green lined by mellow old houses. On Saturday afternoons in summer you can watch a game of cricket. Across the Thames from Kew is charming *Strand-on-the-Green*, and other pleasant Thames-side villages are found at *Twickenham* and *Chiswick*. In south London, *Dulwich* has a fine art gallery.

SIGHTSEEING BY LONDON TRANSPORT ● London's efficient transportation system of buses and underground trains serves not only the central district but the suburbs as well. On day trips you can visit such destinations as Greenwich, Richmond and Kew, Hampton Court, and Epping Forest.

Several special touring tickets are available for visitors. Information can be obtained at the London Transport office at 55 Broadway, London S.W.1 (above the St. James's Park Underground station) from 9 A.M. to 5 P.M. weekdays, 9 A.M. to 12 noon Saturdays.

HISTORIC HOUSES, CASTLES & GARDENS ● Hundreds of Britain's country homes, castles, and gardens are open to the public. Some are privately owned; others are maintained by the National Trust. A guide to these buildings and gardens is *Historic Houses, Castles & Gardens in Great Britain and Ireland* (published annually by Index Publishers, 30 Finsbury Square, London E.C.2). The guide lists by county all houses, castles, and gardens regularly open to the public, with visiting hours, admission fees, and directions for reaching by public transportation.

ON FOOT IN BRITAIN ● The English countryside is ideal for the casual or experienced walker—for an afternoon's stroll, a weekend excursion, or an extended trek. Public footpaths cut across fields and hills, parallel meandering streams, and take you along narrow, traffic-free lanes. Inns and small hotels provide meals, refreshments, and overnight accommodations.

If a walking trip appeals to you, investigate membership in the Ramblers' Association, 1/4 Crawford Mews, York Street, London, W1H 1PT. The organization does not plan trips, but it advises members on walking possibilities, issues an annual *Bed, Breakfast & Bus Guide*, and has a map library from which members may borrow Ordnance Survey maps. For information on organized walking holidays, write to Ramblers' Association Services Ltd., 1 Crawford Mews, York Street, London W.1, or to the Youth Hostels Association, 29 John Adam Street, London, W.C. 2.

ENGLAND FOR GARDENERS ● Spring is the time for idea-collecting gardeners to see England at its blooming best. Throughout Britain, many public and private gardens are open to visitors. You'll find them listed, with visiting hours, in *Historic Houses, Castles & Gardens.*

In London, flower-lovers will head for Hyde Park, Holland Park, and Kensington Gardens. The big Chelsea Flower Show is held annually the third week of May on the grounds of the Royal Hospital in Chelsea. Other fine gardens near the capital are the Royal Botanic Gardens at Kew, the Gardening Center, Ltd. in Syon Park, and the gardens at Hampton Court Palace, all west of London along the Thames River; and the Wisley Garden of the Royal Horticultural Society at Wisley (Surrey), south of London.

In the countryside, seek out Bodnant Garden at Tal-y-Cafn, Denbighshire, Wales; Hidcote Manor, northeast of Chipping Campden in Gloucestershire; the Sissinghurst Castle gardens, near the village of Sissinghurst, Kent; and the Savill Garden at Windsor Great Park, Berkshire.

In late April and early May, bulb fields transform the Lincolnshire countryside around Spaulding into a bright carpet. Just outside Spaulding is Springfields, the show garden of the British Bulb Industry.

ADMISSION TICKET ● If you plan to visit a number of Britain's castles, gardens, museums and stately homes, inquire about a season ticket covering admission to more than 400 major attractions. In London you can buy the ticket at the British Tourist Authority office, 64 St. James's Street, S.W.1; in the U.S., tickets are available by mail from Britrail Travel International, Inc., 270 Madison Avenue, New York, N.Y. 10016, or from the British Travel Bookshop (address on page 12).

HOME OF GOLF ● Traveling golfers can pit their skills against such famed Scottish courses as St. Andrews, Gleneagles, or Muirfield. Most courses welcome visitors without any introduction formalities and at remarkably moderate cost. For more information and a directory, write to the British Tourist Authority.

FOREST RETREAT ● Semi-wild ponies roam freely and deer graze among the shady groves of oak and beech in the New Forest, once the private game preserve of William the Conqueror. Rich in animal and bird life, the nature reserve provides a pleasant respite from busy touring. Located west of Southampton in Hampshire, the forest is still Crown property but is open to visitors who enjoy walking its winding footpaths and exploring its small villages. Stay in an inn, request a picnic lunch, purchase a map, and strike off for the day along one of the brookside paths that lace the woods and heath.

British Tourist Authority offices
680 Fifth Avenue, New York, N.Y. 10019
875 North Michigan Avenue, Chicago, Ill. 60611
612 South Flower Street, Los Angeles, Calif. 90017

Ireland's friendly West Country

The quiet land—from the River Shannon to Galway Bay

Travelers who visit Ireland's West Country carry away two special memories: the hearty welcome and hospitality of the people, and the peaceful and uncrowded countryside. If you will be landing at Shannon Airport, this trip is a splendid way to begin—or renew—your acquaintance with Ireland. You can attend a medieval banquet, drive along wild coastline, explore a curious lunar-like region, and cruise on the River Shannon.

For a fine beginning, attend one of the medieval castle banquets at any of three restored castles: Bunratty, Knappogue, and Dunguaire. Colleens in 15th century dress greet you. You're served a fine dinner based on authentic recipes, then entertained with Irish ballads, dance, drama, and pageantry. Or you can have a country-style evening with a dinner in a cottage in Bunratty Folk Village, followed by simple songs, dancing, and story-telling. For more information, see page 33.

Bunratty Castle, located a few miles east of Shannon Airport, is open to visitors. In addition to the castle, you can visit Bunratty Folk Village, which contains typically furnished farmhouses and cottages from throughout the region. A blacksmith toils at his forge, women bake Irish soda bread, and you can watch demonstrations of basket weaving and candle making.

From Shannon to Galway Bay

From Shannon Airport you head northwest across County Clare toward the coast. Near Newmarket-on-Fergus is thousand-year-old Dromoland Castle, now a luxury hotel; a side road leads to the ruins of Quin Abbey and to Knappogue Castle with its medieval banquets.

The abbey at Ennis, founded in 1241, contains some unusual sculptures. At Corofin you may see a thatcher putting a new straw roof on a cottage. You can rent a thatched cottage here or in Ballyvaughan (see page 33).

Several miles northwest of Killinaboy is partly-ruined Lemaneagh Castle, a 15th-century tower castle with slit windows. Added to the castle two hundred years later was a four-storied, fortified house.

Golfers may recognize the name of Lahinch with its famous course near the sea. Follow the coast road around Liscannor Bay to the dramatic Cliffs of Moher, rising vertically from the Atlantic in a five-mile wall. One of the best views is from the northern end, where the cliffs reach their maximum height of 668 feet.

Ireland's favorite spa, Lisdoonvarna, is at its liveliest following the harvest. Just beyond it you enter a strange, hilly, limestone desert known as The Burren. Here earlier inhabitants left stone forts and a number of dolmens. Although barren in appearance, this stark geologic area contains rare plants. Numerous caves and underground passageways tunnel beneath the surface.

The main highway—known as the Corkscrew Road—goes northeast to Ballyvaughan, on the shore of Galway

Highway sign in Gaelic and English directs motorists near Lemaneagh Castle, an important O'Brien stronghold.

Athlone (top) on the River Shannon is a boating center. Cruisers can be chartered by the week (right), or you might prefer to rent a thatched cottage in the West Country, such as this one at Ballyvaughan (bottom left). Well-preserved Quin Abbey (center), east of Ennis, was once a Franciscan friary.

May to October you can visit the Yeats Museum at Ballycastle (Thoor Ballylee) southwest of Kinvara, located in the former home of poet-playwright William Butler Yeats.

You can easily explore the city of Galway on foot; begin your walking tour at Eyre Square, with its landscaped memorial garden to the late President Kennedy. Shoppers will find a wide selection of Irish tweeds and hand-knit sweaters from the Aran Islands.

Excursions from Galway

In this land of contrasts, you can sample several different regions during a short visit.

Thirty miles out to sea lie the bleak Aran Islands, home of sturdy subsistence farmers and hardy fishermen, who fish the Atlantic in the traditional *currachs*. The islanders preserve many Gaelic traits, including the language, although they speak English with visitors. Local dress has not changed in centuries, and women spin wool and weave their own material. You take a ferry steamer from Galway to Kilronan on Inishmore, or fly from Shannon or Galway via Aer Arann.

The scenic extravagance of the wild, lonely Connemara country northwest of Galway has attracted numerous painters and poets. The shore is indented by numerous inlets, dotted with islands. Lakes and streams are everywhere, dominated by a rocky mountain range known as the Twelve Bens. You may see some sturdy little Connemara ponies or pass turf-cutters chopping bricks of peat (for fuel) from the bog and stacking it to dry in the wind and sun.

Lough Corrib, north of Galway, is one of the best fishing lakes in Ireland. You can rent boats in Oughterard,

one of the main angling centers. The wooded islands in the lake have ruins and are fun to explore.

From the west country you can cut across County Galway to Athlone and the River Shannon.

Along the Shannon

Athlone lies deep in the Irish midlands near the geographic center of Ireland. Next to Limerick, it is the chief town on the river and a center for boating.

Of all the ways to tour Ireland, few are as relaxing and reveal the countryside as well as a cruise on the Shannon. Several companies operate cruises on the river. For a truly relaxing visit, charter a cruiser for a week (see page 33). Along the Shannon's 150 miles of cruising waters, you see sheep and cattle grazing knee-deep in grass, swans nesting in reeds beside low banks, and tidy stone cottages with slate or thatch roofs. The river widens into three large, shallow, island-studded lakes.

Remains of Ireland's most famous monastic settlement, Clonmacnois, lie beside the Shannon south of Athlone. Founded in the 6th century and often the object of plundering raids, the site contains many ruined buildings.

Continuing south, you cross to the river's west bank at Banagher and follow along Lough Derg, the finest of the Shannon's lakes, popular with fishermen, sailors, and waterskiers. You'll have fine views south to Killaloe.

Although Limerick is a regional market and industrial center, many of its historic buildings have been preserved. Making Limerick lace is still a home industry, and you'll find lacework in some of the local stores. Limerick's history dates to the 9th century, when Viking raiders sailed up the Shannon and used the site as a base for plundering the prosperous countryside.

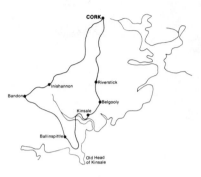

Touring by gypsy caravan

You meet the Irish when you travel by horse-drawn wagon

What better way to get acquainted with the "oul' sod" than to travel through the south and west of Ireland in a horse-drawn gypsy caravan? You can cover about 12 miles in a day of leisurely travel, bedding down for the night wherever you like.

As your horse plods through the low, rolling green hills and along peaceful country lanes, you see the Irish countryside close up. Wave at travelers you pass, stop to chat with farmers, buy your food along the route, and in the evenings seek out the friendly village pubs where you are readily included in lively conversation.

Gaily painted caravans (covered wagons) can be rented by the week in several areas of Ireland, but no region is more ideally suited to this pleasant, unhurried way of travel than County Cork.

Your caravan may not have all the conveniences of a modern house trailer, but the facilities are comfortable and more than adequate for a leisurely one or two-week tour through the Irish countryside. A rental fee of about $100 a week (higher in July and August) includes a fully-equipped caravan with a canvas top and rubber-tired wheels, a gentle dray horse, bottled gas for cooking and lighting, and insurance coverage.

Most caravans will sleep four or five persons. A caravan for four includes a double bed that converts to a dining table and benches during the day, along with two single bunks that can be made up into a settee. You prepare meals on a two-burner stove and wash dishes in a small sink. Water is drawn from a refillable 5-gallon plastic container. Ample bedding, dishes, and kitchen equipment come with the caravan; check to see if you need to bring towels. Provisions and dishes fits into cupboards, and bedding is stored under the bunks. A full-length hanging closet and other open storage shelves and cupboards are fitted in wherever there is room.

Planning your trip

Ireland is warm enough for caravan touring from April through September, with ever-changing skies and at least a half dozen kinds of weather possible in a 24-hour period. The climate is mild and showery, but rain clouds blow over quickly. Summer temperatures vary between 60 and 70 degrees.

Wear trousers and sweaters, take along shorts and a bathing suit, and most important of all, don't overlook light rain gear. At almost any village store you can buy farmers' black rubber boots. Worn with a pair of woolen socks, they make ideal footgear.

Before leaving Cork, stock the cupboards with provisions to last about 2 days. Often you can purchase fresh eggs, brown bread, and vegetables at overnight stops along the way. Village stores are open 7 days a week. Even in small villages you can buy pasteurized milk, butter, cheese, meat, fruit, vegetables, and bread.

The rental company will help you plan your trip. Operators can suggest itineraries which will avoid heavy traffic and steep hills, farms where you can purchase food or arrange to pasture your horse for the night. Some operators will rent bicycles or an extra riding horse.

Two caravans travel toward Cork along the Dripsey road. Van trip is a favorite holiday of many English families.

Your horse becomes an important member of your group. Harnessing and driving instructions are given before starting out (top left); no previous experience is necessary. Teenager prepares dinner for the horse — a quart of oats (bottom left). Portable steps provide access to wagon. At right, a caravan approaches the wide sandy beach of Garrettstown.

County Cork lends itself to caravan travel, with long, level stretches of roadway, low rolling hills, and comparatively few automobiles.

Few organized trailer parks exist in uncrowded Ireland, but "no trespassing" signs are rare, and you can park in almost any pleasant site you find. (When you are obviously on privately-owned land, be sure to ask permission at the nearest farmhouse.)

Before you start out, purchase a detailed road map from an Irish Tourist Board booth or from a Cork service station. All main roads are numbered, with distances between towns given in miles. Both T (Trunk or main) and L (Link or secondary) roads are usually hard-surfaced, although most roads are only two lanes wide.

Meeting your horse

To begin your new career as an Irish gypsy, you must select and get acquainted with your horse. The caravan operator will instruct you in the harnessing, feeding, and grooming procedure. When you have had some practical experience in placing the horse between the shafts and coupling him to the wagon, one of the grooms will ride with you to the outskirts of town. If you need a quick refresher course on the harnessing sequence, look for instructions placed in each caravan. Assistance will be given at official overnight stops.

Although horses are completely familiar with traffic and exhibit no skittish tendencies, each one has his own personality. Should you need some help along the way, you won't have to look far. Since most Irishmen are horse fanciers, your horse-drawn caravan will be more impressive than a letter of introduction when you meet farmers and villagers.

On the road

Your route through County Cork leads to simple, unspoiled villages with delightful names like Belgooly, Ballinspittle, and Ballinadee. Except on weekends, country roads are nearly free of traffic. One or more of your party may prefer to walk beside the caravan, while those riding can brew a cup of tea or fix a sandwich even as the wagon is moving.

At the end of each day, look for a good fenced pasture for the horse (inquire at a village store, farm cottage, or pub), water and feed him, then turn him loose to graze. From a 10 or 20-pound sack of oats bought at the beginning of the trip, give the horse about a quart of oats three times a day. Farmers along the route will usually pasture your horse overnight for a nominal charge, help you with unharnessing and harnessing, and perhaps sell you fresh eggs, butter, homemade soda bread, and vegetables. Wherever you stop, inquire about the nearest source of fresh water — pump or tap. Arrange with a neighboring farmer for the use of his plumbing facilities.

In the evenings you'll find a friendly welcome in the local pub, or, for a change of pace, you may decide to have dinner in a wayside inn or resort.

Operators of horse-drawn caravans are based in the following counties: Cork, Kerry, Leitrim, Limerick, Mayo, and Wicklow. Addresses of the companies are available from the Irish Tourist Board; for more information, write to the caravan operator.

Into the Wicklow Mountains

Lush river valleys cut between the granite peaks

Ireland creates much beauty for export—Irish linen, Belleek china, Waterford crystal. But the best of Ireland can't be shipped abroad. It has to be visited to be seen, and a good place to begin is the Wicklow Mountains.

Less than an hour's drive south of Dublin, this is a region of haunting beauty, wooded valleys and dark lakes tucked between domed granite mountains. Streams tumble down the hillsides and cut through remote valleys. In the foothills charming villages tempt you to linger. You may even decide to rent a horse for a few hours of riding (see page 32).

Painters continually try to capture the changing colors of the hills—shades of brown flecked with the greyish white of granite outcrops, the greens of forest and field, purple heather, and golden gorse. Fishermen test their skills in the clear streams; hikers and riders explore the quiet paths and trails.

South from Dublin

Enniskerry, one of Ireland's most charming villages, lies about 12 miles south of Dublin in a wooded hollow among the northern foothills of the Wicklow Mountains. About a mile east you'll find the wooded Glen of the Dargle River, a ravine where the narrowing valley restricts the waters to a rushing torrent.

From Easter to October you can visit Powerscourt, an elegant 14,000-acre estate along the River Dargle near Enniskerry. Noted for its terraced gardens, the estate has a long main drive that runs beside the river through a deer park to Powerscourt Waterfall, formed as the river tumbles 400 feet over a cliff. The mansion was recently destroyed by fire.

The Glencree road climbs west from Enniskerry to connect with the north-south Military Road. For centuries the Wicklow Mountains were the stronghold of the unsubdued O'Tooles and O'Byrnes, and the British built the road after the Insurrection of 1798 for use by the 'redcoats' in their pursuit of the Wicklowmen. Today the Military Road opens up for motorists the lonely, mysterious moorlands, several mountain tarns, and the summit of Kippure. You pass near the source of the River Liffey, then cut through the Sally Gap (1,631 feet). Below, in a deep eastern valley, lie Loughs Tay and Dan.

Bleak moorlands suddenly give way to the dramatic Valley of Glenmacnass, walled in by towering mountains, and you drive along the river to Laragh, the gateway to Glendalough.

Wild and historic Glendalough

Several glens and roads converge at Laragh. Westward stretches Glendalough, the Valley of Two Lakes, famed

Glendalough is one of Ireland's most beautiful valleys. Round tower and other monastic ruins date from the 7th century.

Sheep are driven to new pastureland in the mountains (top). You drive beside the Avonmore River through the lovely Vale of Clara (bottom left). St. Kevin's Church, with its steeply-pitched stone roof, is one of the best-preserved ruins at Glendalough (center). Powerscourt estate near Enniskerry has elegant gardens (right).

both for its wild beauty and its historical and archeological interest. Steep hills hem in the valley, but you'll find good walking trails.

Ruins lying around the lakes' shores are the remnants of a great monastic city in the valley, once renowned as one of the great learning centers of Europe. You can trace the history of the glen from the ruins — from its founding as a monastery in the 6th century by St. Kevin, through its golden age, its plundering by the Vikings and later invaders, down to 1398, when it was finally burned and left deserted.

The gateway to the area was the original entrance to the monastic city. Although the cathedral is now in ruins, St. Kevin's Church — an example of early Irish barrel-vaulted oratories with its stone, high-pitched roof — is well preserved.

The Round Tower, still in almost perfect condition after more than a thousand years, stands 110 feet high and 52 feet in circumference at the base. Its small doorway 11½ feet from the ground was reached by ladder, drawn up behind the monks in time of attack.

Wooded river valleys

South of Laragh, the Military Road climbs again into the hills, then drops down into wild Glenmalure, flanked by mountains including 3,039-foot Lugnaquilla, highest of the Wicklow Mountains. Scenic side roads branch off to the valley of the Avonbeg River. Five miles south of Glenmalure, the Military Road ends at Aughavannagh.

Turn southeast along the river road to Aughrim and continue beside the trout-filled Aughrim River to Woodenbridge, attractively situated at the junction of three valleys. Gold mines operated near here beginning in 1796, and other ore deposits in the district — copper, lead, zinc, and sulphur — were known in Roman times.

In late spring the Vale of Avoca is especially colorful, the white blossoms of wild cherry trees standing out against the green countryside. Many travelers journey to the attractive riverside park north of Avoca, a setting made famous in the poem *Meeting of the Waters* by Thomas Moore. Here the Avonmore and Avonbeg rivers converge.

Continue north to the little town of Rathdrum, along the Avonmore River through the Vale of Clara, and up to Laragh.

The Georgian charm of Blessington

If time permits, drive west from Laragh through the Wicklow Gap to Hollywood, turning north to Blessington. This pleasant village typifies the restful, rural charm of Ireland's small towns. In the days of horse-drawn mail coaches, it served as a staging post on the route from Dublin south to Carlow, Kilkenny, and Waterford. The Georgian façades along its long, wide, tree-lined main street reflect that more leisurely era.

East of the village is Poulaphouca Lake, not only the source of Dublin's hydro-electric power and water supply but also the site of recreational facilities.

Pony-trekking in Ireland

Rent a horse for an afternoon's ride in the countryside

Riding a horse through the Irish countryside lets you enjoy the lushness of the country slowly and in detail. You wander down lanes where cars never go, stop to chat with passersby, or canter over the green hills.

It's surprisingly easy to arrange horseback trips in Ireland. The riding enthusiast is never far from a stable where he can hire a mount for an afternoon's ride through pleasant woods or hills. Organized pony-trek-

Riders return *from an afternoon's canter through the wooded Irish countryside. Horseback trips are simple to arrange.*

king holidays are available in many parts of the Irish countryside.

You don't need to be an expert horseman to sample the joys of cantering over Ireland's hills or ambling along a woodland path. Novice riders can take a riding lesson before starting out on a short excursion. The groom will suggest routes to fit your ability and time. Often stables have ponies available for children.

Rent a horse by the hour (called "hacking" by the Irish) or for a half day or full day. An hour's riding instruction costs about $4 per person. The charge for an hour's hacking is about $4, while a full day's trek costs approximately $10.

If you ride fairly well, you can arrange to go out with a group on a pony trek. Such a trek consists of a small group of riders with a guide who spend about six hours on horseback, returning to a base in the evening. Most riding centers either supply a box lunch to carry along or arrange for riders to take a midday meal in a cottage or farmhouse.

Extended pony-trekking tours are also available, all-inclusive charges covering accommodations, horse, guide, lunches, and five days of trekking.

For additional information on riding in Ireland and a list of riding schools, stables, and agencies that arrange pony-trekking excursions, write to the Irish Tourist Board (address on page 33).

If you prefer to watch

If you're not up to riding, you can watch Ireland's horses in a variety of events. In a country where horse racing is the national pastime, you'll find plenty of opportunities to see the handsome animals in action; check the calendar of events for a list of races.

Many towns and villages hold gymkhanas during the summer. You can watch polo matches in summer on Wednesdays and Saturdays at Dublin's Phoenix Park.

Highlight of the horseman's year, the Dublin Horse Show, comes during the first week of August. More than 2,000 horses are entered in the show.

Market day in Concarneau is a lively affair, where grandmothers in lacy coiffes (left) mingle with blue-garbed fishermen and vegetable farmers.
Strange megaliths at Carnac are arranged in long, parallel rows (right), one of several places in Brittany where ancient stone monuments may be seen.

Sturdy ramparts surround the Ville Close, an irregularly-shaped island separating the island's inner and outer harbor. Laced with narrow alleys, the island is fun to explore—from the ramparts you have a view of harbor and fleet. In summer a fishing museum is open.

There's usually some activity along Concarneau's quays, and early risers can visit the 7 A.M. fish market on weekdays along the inner harbor quay. On Monday and Friday mornings, women from surrounding villages flock to town to buy vegetables in the marketplace, along with clothing, household utensils, and perhaps even baby chicks and ducks.

A few miles below Concarneau is Pont-Aven, a pleasant little town favored by painters. Paul Gauguin was a member of the local artists' colony in the late 1880s. A small museum displays paintings by Gauguin and the Pont-Aven group (open summers only). Quimperlé's unusual Church of Ste. Croix is built on the same plan as the Church of the Holy Sepulchre in Jerusalem. Hennebont, located upriver from the industrial port and naval base at Lorient, has remnants of its fortified town.

In 1776 a ship carrying Benjamin Franklin on his way to negotiate a treaty with France landed at Auray when it was unable to sail up the Loire River to Nantes. Auray's quay is named for Franklin; a plaque marks the house where he stayed. A wooded hillside overlooks the port, houses of the St. Goustan Quarter, and the river.

Prehistoric stone markers

Among Brittany's most distinctive characteristics are the great prehistoric monuments scattered over the countryside. More than 3,000 giant stones can still be seen around Carnac and Locmariaquer, placed by a little-known race between 3500 and 1800 B.C.

Single stones (called *menhirs*), often over 20 feet high and weighing up to 350 tons, were set up near ancient tombs and on slopes of hills. The largest was the Great Menhir, in the village of Locmariaquer, now broken in several pieces but once some 75 feet long.

Dolmens were probably burial chambers, a circle of parallel rows of upright stones topped by a flat slab. Originally they were buried under mounds of dry stones or earth, called *tumuli*. In the same clearing as the Great Menhir you'll see the Merchants' Table dolmen, partially covered by a tumulus, with carved designs on the inside.

You'll also see lines of menhirs, probably the remains of ancient religious monuments. The greatest display is north of Carnac, called the Alignements of Ménec, where more than a thousand menhirs were arranged in parallel rows, covering an area 100 yards wide and ¾ mile long. Running from east to west (apparently placed to coincide with the lines of sunrise and sunset at the summer and winter solstices), they end in a semi-circle of giant stones.

Southwest of Carnac, the Quiberon Peninsula is a former island connected to the mainland by a narrow corridor of land. You can walk or drive along the western shore, known as the Côte Sauvage (Wild Coast) and indented by rocky cliffs and grottos. Steamers leave Quiberon for the island of Belle-Ile.

The Gulf of Morbihan

A small island-dotted inland sea lies south of Vannes, its inlets and tidal estuaries cutting deeply into the interior. At high tide the sparkling sea surrounds numerous islands, but at low tide, broad mud banks spread between the river channels.

Many fishing boats and pleasure craft sail among the islands, for the best way to see the Gulf of Morbihan is by boat. In summer, boat trips are available.

Vannes has an attractive old quarter, grouped around the cathedral and partially enclosed by ramparts. The park of the former castle is a garden and promenade.

EUROPE'S MARVELOUS OPEN-AIR MARKETS

Open-air markets offer a special way to discover a country and its people. Often much more exciting than visiting monuments and museums, sampling Europe's outdoor markets offers a colorful, noisy, fragrant, good-humored view of a city. Products on sale reflect regional tastes, and friendliness usually accompanies business transactions.

Nearly every city and large town has at least one market, its origin going back centuries to when farmers brought surplus vegetables and fruits to the city to sell. Markets may operate nearly every day of the week in large cities, but in most towns, market day comes once or twice a week — occasions when the happy atmosphere of a local fair prevails.

You'll probably discover some of the best local markets by accident. If you maintain a flexible schedule, you'll have time to stroll through the stalls and enjoy the colorful activity.

Produce markets • The most frequently found markets — those selling vegetables and fruit — exist in most major towns. Merchants set up displays on portable tables or spread boxes and baskets beneath striped or brightly colored awnings and umbrellas. Housewives, armed with huge shopping baskets and bags, take their time deciding what to buy. Often fresh flowers are sold, and in rural towns you'll find clothing, garden plants, and household utensils, as well. Market day is a social time to meet friends, to exchange local news, and (in some towns) to dress in traditional costumes.

Sometimes the bustle of the marketplace leads you to the site, often near the town hall or main church. Your hotel concierge or the local tourist office can direct you.

Some of the classic city markets have disappeared under the guise of progress, but you can still delight in — among others — Palermo's Vucceria, the elegant Boqueria market of Barcelona, Munich's Viktualienmarkt, and the crowded Rue Mouffetard of Paris.

Flower markets • Sometimes part of the produce market, and sometimes separate. Brilliant bouquets of cut flowers delight the eye. Potted plants and nursery stock are sometimes also sold.

Food markets • You have to get up early to visit London's Billingsgate (fish and shellfish) or Smithfield (meat), but they're traditions. Sausages decorate stands in Germanic markets. In autumn, wild game assumes an honored place. Glistening, freshly caught fish are sold at market or auction in many harbor towns. Holland cheese markets draw many visitors. For an offbeat market, visit the Italian town of Alba in the Piedmont region during the October truffle fair.

Bird and animal markets • In several cities, Sunday bird markets unite children with feathered friends. In rural centers — and surprisingly, in several major cities as well — regular markets satisfy the trade in cattle, sheep, pigs, and chickens.

Flea markets • Almost every large city has a flea market, where anything and everything is displayed for bargain hunters. Some are open daily, others just on weekends.

Hobby markets • Craft bazaars and art shows pop up as a feature of local markets and fairs. In Paris you can visit a stamp market or one specializing in sewing fabrics and notions. Brussels has a weekend antiques and book market.

Lively outdoor markets display a colorful variety of products: (left to right) vegetables and flowers in Lucerne, Switzerland; crab and squid in Venice, Italy; round, golden cheeses in Alkmaar, Holland.

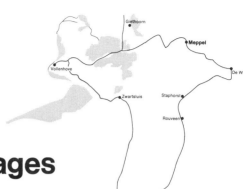

Two unusual Overijssel villages

Go "punting" in Giethoorn and visit intriguing Staphorst

A pair of intriguing villages lie off the main roads in quiet northwest Overijssel. All traffic goes by boat in canal-cut Giethoorn. Ultra-religious Staphorst is known for unusual customs, bright farmhouses, and costumes.

Start your excursion in Zwolle, at the crossroads of trade routes between Holland and northern Germany. Villagers from outlying districts are lured to the big Friday market here. In one place you can see the lace-capped women from the Veluwe district, Staphorst farmers and their wives, and the fisher-folk of Urk.

Formerly a walled city, the town still has numerous 15th-century buildings, but its ramparts have been leveled to form lawns and flower beds.

North of Zwolle lies the water sports district of Salland. Once a busy fishing port, Vollenhove was cut off from open water by the completed North-East Polder.

Boating on Giethoorn's canals

The rustic village of Giethoorn is in a class by itself. There are no streets in this charming hamlet, only shallow canals shaped by peat-diggers three centuries ago. All traffic goes by boat (photo on back cover). Flat-bottomed boats called "punters" transport cows to and from pasture, the postman on his route, villagers to Sunday church. Each house sits among trees on its own island, reached by boat or wooden footbridge.

You can make arrangements for a boat and a pilot to guide you through this maze of canals, past thatched cottages and beneath bridges. Sometimes shy children peek out to watch you glide by.

Farmers and their wives gather on Thursday mornings for the weekly market in Meppel, another market town in this rich agricultural area. From early July to mid-August, dance groups add to the festive air.

The unusual village of Staphorst

Put away your camera as you approach the village of Staphorst, known throughout Holland for its strict Calvinist religious beliefs, colorful painted farmhouses and furniture, costumes, and intense dislike of prying pho-

tographers. Visitors are tolerated as unavoidable annoyances, but photography is resented to the degree that it is prohibited by local law. Visitors are particularly unwelcome on Sundays, when the Sabbath is strictly observed.

Yet the village follows the unusual custom of trial maternity. No young man will marry a local girl until she can prove she can keep his farm supplied with children, for all work is done by members of the family.

Stop at the Hotel Waanders to see some of the Staphorst painted furniture. Behind the hotel is a farmhouse, also furnished in old Staphorst style and open to visitors. More colorful houses, trimmed in brilliant green and blue, line the road south to Rouveen.

Flat-bottomed boats *transport people, animals, and provisions along Giethoorn's tree-shaded waterways.*

South to watery Zeeland

You're never far from water in southwestern Holland

South of Rotterdam on Holland's southwest coast, a massive engineering project is closing out the North Sea. By the end of the decade, the 25-year Delta Project will be completed, damming the long arms of the sea which cut deeply into Zeeland. Ultimately the estuaries will be transformed into fresh-water lakes.

Zeeland is a quiet, rural land. Most of its people are hard-working farmers, somewhat removed from world events. Local market days are colorful and lively; a number of shoppers wear their traditional costumes.

South Beveland women, *identified as Protestants by close-fitting bonnets, walk briskly down brick-paved road.*

You can enjoy the Zeeland towns and countryside on a one or two-day excursion from Rotterdam. In summer the Netherlands Railways schedules independent day excursions to Zeeland and to the Delta Works (see page 63), and summer boat trips to the Delta Works leave from Rotterdam and Hellevoetsluis. Check with the Rotterdam V. V. V. office (19 Stadhuisplein) for the current schedule.

The Delta Project

Over the centuries the Dutch have wrested much of their land from the sea. But the most extensive work ever undertaken is the Delta Project, now in progress in Zeeland.

Preliminary studies had already begun but were spurred on by the tragic Zeeland floods of 1953, when over 375,000 acres were flooded. Hundreds of people lost their lives, more than 70,000 people had to be evacuated, and damage reached nearly half a billion dollars. Large breaches in the dikes had to be repaired, polders drained, houses and villages restored.

All of the plans for protecting the southwest against future floods were merged into a single gigantic plan— the Delta Project. When the project is completed early in the 1980s, dams will shut out the North Sea. Lakes formed behind the dams will gradually change to fresh water, increasing the area's recreational opportunities. Waterways leading to the ports of Rotterdam and Antwerp will remain open to ship traffic.

Zeeland's villages and beaches

South from Rotterdam on the Delta route, you cross Zeeland's wide estuaries on a series of bridges and atop dams. First comes Haringvliet Bridge, completed in 1967. You cross the island of Goeree-Overflakkee to the next estuary; here the highway continues atop the Grevelingedam, ushering you into Zeeland and the island of Schouwen-Duiveland.

A 16th-century mood permeates Zierikzee, the island's

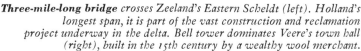

Three-mile-long bridge crosses Zeeland's Eastern Scheldt (left). Holland's longest span, it is part of the vast construction and reclamation project underway in the delta. Bell tower dominates Veere's town hall (right), built in the 15th century by a wealthy wool merchant.

main town. On a stroll you'll find beautiful old houses, ancient city gates, the old port, and the town hall with a regional museum. If you're in town on Thursday, wander through the local market.

You go through several villages on a loop trip around the island. Dreischor has one central building containing town hall, school, church, and fire station. The port of Brouwershaven has an interesting town hall. On the western tip, Haamstede and Westenschouwen are starting points for walks in the wooded dunes and quiet beaches. Because the wind from the North Sea is brisk, you'll find no crowds here.

South of Zierikzee you cross the Eastern Scheldt on Holland's longest bridge, the Zeelandbrug.

Exploring Walcheren

Families who love water sports head for the former island of Walcheren, one of Holland's favorite coastal holiday areas. Here they can sail, fish, and water-ski in the Veerse Meer, a former estuary now enclosed to form a fresh-water lake. Walcheren's south-facing beaches are sheltered from the cold sea winds. From them, you can watch ocean-going vessels cruise along the Western Scheldt to and from the Belgian port of Antwerp.

Walcheren was occupied and fortified by the Nazis in 1940. After the Normandy landings, the Allies needed the port of Antwerp to unload supplies, so Walcheren's dikes were bombed to flood the Nazis out. Reclamation was a tremendous task, but finally the land was made productive again – until the floods of 1953.

Veere, on the island's northeast rim, is Walcheren's most historic town. During the days of the 16th-century wool trade, it was ten times its present size. Raw wool was shipped here from Scotland, then sent on to Flemish

merchants in Bruges, Belgium, to be made into fine cloth. Today Veere is a yacht harbor and water sports center, its streets and quays bordered by rich buildings.

Veere's town hall was built by the wealthy Van Borselen family, who had exclusive rights to the Scottish wool trade; they decorated the exterior with statues of members of the family. They also started construction of the huge church, but it was too ambitious and expensive a project. Napoleon used the church as a hospital for his troops in 1811, adding four new floors to house patients.

Middelburg and the beaches

Badly damaged by bombs in 1940, Middelburg has been rebuilt and restored. Near its fine town hall is a small war museum, containing a model showing the innundation and reclamation of Walcheren. A relief map of the island shows towns, dikes, and fields; you watch water pour in through the breaches, see the dikes closed up, and the water dry away.

Another favorite attraction for both children and adults is Miniature Walcheren, small-size replicas of the island's villages and towns, canals and harbors, roads and beaches, ships and trains – even a dredging machine.

From Middelburg you can make a circuit of the beaches: the family resort of Domburg, Westkapelle with many reminders of the Nazi occupation and bombing, and the southern beach resorts between Zouteland and Vlissingen.

Head east from Vlissingen across polderland and through fruit orchards to Goes, main city of South Beveland. On Tuesday afternoons women from nearby villages gather for the weekly market.

Sampling Luxembourg

You can see the entire country in just a few days

You can tour the entire Grand Duchy of Luxembourg, one of Europe's smaller countries, in two or three days, or you can make it a restful stopover and do your sightseeing in a more leisurely manner. Luxembourg's central location — bordered on the west by Belgium, on the east by Germany, and on the south by France — makes it easy to include in your itinerary.

From the capital city, also named Luxembourg, a circuit covers a variety of landscapes — the vineyard district along the Moselle, the wild rocky region known as "Little Switzerland," and the forested mountains and wild rivers of the Ardennes. Luxembourg is walkers' country, and footpaths head into the woods or along rivers from most major towns (see page 63).

The thousand-year-old fortress city of Luxembourg, with its towers and pointed roofs, perches atop a rocky cliff, dominating the river valley and newer town below. At night the old town is floodlighted. Wednesday and Saturday are the city's market days. The capital is the home of H.R.H. the Grand Duke; his palace, guarded by uniformed soldiers, is often photographed by visitors.

Along the Moselle

Luxembourg's vineyards are located on hills along the Moselle river, on the country's southeastern border. From spring through fall you can visit a number of cellars between the towns of Remich and Grevenmacher, perhaps buying a bottle of the delicate white wine to go with a picnic lunch of smoked Ardennes ham. Canal boats ply the Moselle, fishermen test their skills in its waters, and walkers enjoy tree-shaded walks along the river's banks.

Echternach and Berdorf are favorite summer resorts near the entrance of Luxembourg's "Little Switzerland," a wild and rocky region of wooded ravines and unusual rock formations. Dozens of footpaths crisscross the wooded hills and valleys, leading to waterfalls, rocks, and scenic viewpoints. You can also fish, canoe, or go rockclimbing. The drive through the Mullertal, along the valley of the Ernz Noir, is particularly beautiful.

North to the Ardennes

The northern part of the country is a recreation-oriented region of forested hills cut by fast-moving rivers. Diekirch is a favorite waterside resort for fishing and canoeing on the River Sûre; you may wish to see well-preserved Roman mosaics and the Celtic dolmen "Devil's Altar" here.

Feudal fortress at Vianden, on Luxembourg's northeastern border, overlooks its town and the valley of the Our.

IN THE LOW COUNTRIES: special interests

HOLLAND BY BICYCLE • Adventuresome — and energetic — visitors can see the country as the Dutch do. Nearly everyone cycles in the Netherlands; the flat, quiet Dutch countryside is ideal for bicycling. Many of the roads have parallel cycle tracks, and attractive cycling routes have been signposted in all parts of the country.

Visitors can rent bicycles by the hour or day at many cycle repair shops and at more than 80 railway stations throughout Holland. Local V.V.V. offices can suggest scenic routes and provide cycling maps.

TOURING BELGIAN CASTLES • Many historic castles in Belgium are open to visitors; some of them are still homes, lived in by descendants of the families who built and furnished them.

For information on castles currently open to the public, visiting hours, and travel directions, write to the Belgian National Tourist Office.

DUTCH WINDMILLS • For many visitors, windmills are a fascinating part of Dutch folklore. About 1,000 windmills still remain in Holland. The Netherlands National Tourist Office publishes a leaflet on the locations of windmills still to be found in Holland, along with a bit of their history and windmill "language."

North of Amsterdam in the Zaan district, a number of mills are located along the Zaan River, and the Zaansch Molen Museum is open afternoons from April through September (closed Mondays and Fridays). Nineteen mills — set in polder landscape at Kinderdijk, east of Rotterdam — operate Saturday afternoons in July and August.

BIRD ISLAND • Each spring over 120 kinds of wild birds migrate to the quiet island of Texel, off the Dutch mainland, to breed and raise their young. Guides conduct human visitors around the bird sanctuaries; the Texel V.V.V. office has a brochure on bird life on the island. Behind the dunes, bulbs bloom in the spring.

Regular ferry service connects the island with the mainland town of Den Helder.

CAMPING IN LUXEMBOURG • Forests and river valleys of Luxembourg are popular with campers. More than a hundred campgrounds offer a variety of activities: boating, hiking, horseback riding, swimming, golf, and tennis. For a list of camping areas, write to the Luxembourg Tourist Office.

LIFE ON A DUTCH FARM • You see cows milked, vegetables and flowers grown, pigs and chickens raised when you spend a day in the country at Flevohof, the national agricultural fair. Visitors are free to roam the fields, greenhouses, and barns, or you can even try your hand at churning butter or sorting eggs. Children have their own special village, where they can bake bread, fry pancakes, or ride ponies. Flevohof, located about 75 miles northeast of Amsterdam, is open daily the year round.

BELGIAN MUSEUM VILLAGE • The open-air museum at Bokrijk recreates the Belgium of centuries past in a park-like setting about 55 miles east of Brussels. Ancient houses surround a triangular village green, sheep graze in the fields, and craftsmen demonstrate the use of farm and household tools. Located between Hasselt and Genk, the provincial reserve also includes an arboretum and garden, lakes, and a deer park. The museum is open from April through October; the park is open all year.

RAIL EXCURSIONS • From April through September, the Netherlands Railways offers a number of all-inclusive excursion tickets to destinations of special interest. For a brochure, write to the Netherlands National Tourist Office.

EVOLUON EXHIBITION • You stroll through the strange world of science and technology in Holland's Evoluon in Eindhoven. Exhibits reveal secrets of nature, the atom, magnetic force, space travel, and other subjects. Visitors can operate some of the exhibits.

MARKED WALKING ROUTES • Luxembourg is walkers' country. A number of marked footpaths, indicated by yellow signs, wind along rivers and through forests. The Luxembourg Tourist Office can provide a list of the routes. Map folders with marked routes are available at local tourist offices.

HOLLAND'S FLORAL HIGHLIGHTS • Springtime in the Netherlands is heralded by bulb fields and orchards in bloom, but colorful floral displays continue through the summer into autumn. For information on floral parades, displays, and posted bulb and blossom routes, write to the Netherlands National Tourist Office.

BELGIAN FESTIVALS • Belgians love festive events, and they participate enthusiastically in carnivals, fetes, and processions throughout the year. Many are based on ancient traditions or folklore. For a listing of festivals and events, write to the Belgian National Tourist Office.

FOLKLORE MARKETS • Each summer a number of Dutch country towns enliven local market days with traditional costumes, craft demonstrations, and village bands and dance groups. Write to the Netherlands National Tourist Office for a list of market towns.

Netherlands National Tourist Offices
576 Fifth Avenue, New York, N.Y. 10017
681 Market Street, San Francisco, Calif. 94105

Belgian National Tourist Office
720 Fifth Avenue, New York, N.Y. 10019

Luxembourg Tourist Office
1 Dag Hammarskjold Plaza, New York, N.Y. 10017

Through Germany's fairy tale land

Wander through medieval towns or go for a walk in the woods

Fetching golden-haired princesses and handsome princes, wicked witches and mean stepmothers, industrious dwarfs and bewitched animals—this cast of characters from the tales of the brothers Grimm sprang from the rolling hill country cut by the Weser River and from the thick forests of the Harz Mountains.

But you'll find much more than legends or fairy tales in this unspoiled region. Medieval towns where you wander freely, country castles and quiet villages, forest hiking trails and wild mountain ravines all wait to be explored.

Weser River winds placidly through the rolling German countryside. Passenger boats cruise the Weser in summer.

Along the Weser

South of Hameln the Weser River winds through fertile fields and between the wooded hills of the Weserbergland. From May to September passenger boats cruise between Hann. Münden and Hameln, and downriver from Hameln as well.

Towns large and small boast fine old houses, both elegant half-timbered buildings and sandstone ones built in the local architectural style known as Weser Renaissance, with characteristic scrollwork and pinnacles on the gables. Weathered pink limestone tiles cover the roofs.

Hameln, built on the right bank of the Weser, occupies a special spot in German folklore. It is the town of that famed ratcatcher, the Pied Piper. The legend is dramatized near the town hall each Sunday at noon from June through August.

In Bodenwerder a museum displays mementoes of the town's best-known resident, the legendary Baron Hieronymus von Münchhausen, called the "Lying Baron" because of his tall tales of adventure. Höxter is a pleasant riverside town, and Fürstenberg is famous for porcelain.

At Karlshafen you have a choice of routes. You can continue up the narrowing Weser valley through quiet villages to Hann. Münden, or take an alternate route through the Reinhardswald to Kassel.

The road through the wooded Reinhardswald, south of Karlshafen, leads to the medieval castles of Trendelburg and Sababurg, both now castle-hotels (see page 75). From its wooded hilltop, Trendelburg Castle overlooks the village. Romantic Sababurg, locally called "Sleeping Beauty's castle," lies northeast of Hofgeismar off the main road, surrounded by virgin forest.

Hann. Münden is situated at the confluence of the Fulda and Werra rivers, which join to form the Weser. The city's old center includes more than 450 old half-timbered houses (*Fachwerkhäuser*).

Brothers Jacob and Wilhelm Grimm lived in Kassel in the early 19th century, working as court librarians while gathering folk tales of the countryside—among them Hansel and Grethel, Snow White, Rumpelstiltskin, and Little Red Riding Hood. A Brothers Grimm Museum

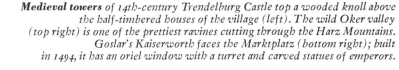

Medieval towers of 14th-century Trendelburg Castle top a wooded knoll above the half-timbered houses of the village (left). The wild Oker valley (top right) is one of the prettiest ravines cutting through the Harz Mountains. Goslar's Kaiserworth faces the Marktplatz (bottom right); built in 1494, it has an oriel window with a turret and carved statues of emperors.

in Bellevue "Schlosschen" contains mementoes (open weekdays from 10 to 6, Saturday and Sunday 10 to 1).

West of Kassel the huge Wilhelmshöhe Castle Park stretches across forested slopes. Park fountains operate in summer on Wednesday, Sunday, and holiday afternoons from 3:30 to 4:30. Schloss Wilhelmshöhe houses a wallpaper museum (open daily except Monday).

The Harz Mountains

From the Weser valley our route heads east to the lively university town of Göttingen, another center of half-timbered houses, and then to the Harz Mountains.

This wild, wooded region tops all the surrounding foothills and spans the border between West and East Germany. Mount Brocken, the highest point, lies in the East Zone. According to legend, on Walpurgis night (April 30) witches astride their broomsticks gather on the summit for a night of revelry.

The Harz is a popular holiday area with visitors who flock to its resorts and spas and hike through its pine forests. Many fine mountain hiking trails begin and end at car parks (see page 75). In winter, snow blankets the meadows and hillsides.

Clausthal-Zellerfeld was once the mining capital of the Upper Harz Mountains; the Zellerfeld museum illustrates some unusual local mining methods. From here you continue to Goslar through the Oker valley, one of the most charming of the Harz ravines.

Medieval Goslar

Of the many old towns at the foot of the Harz, the most important is the imperial city of Goslar, one of Germany's classic medieval cities. You can easily spend a full day exploring this fascinating place.

Once a favorite residence of the emperors of the Holy Roman Empire, Goslar began to boom when rich ore deposits were discovered in the Harz. During the early 16th century, prospering merchants and skilled craftsmen built an impressive town hall, mighty churches, richly decorated guildhalls, and timber-fronted houses ornamented with elaborately carved oriel windows *(Erker)*. Walls and moats, strong towers and gates encircled the town. Goslar's decline began about 1550, and the town remained substantially undisturbed for several hundred years.

Begin your exploration at the dignified Marktplatz, walking past fine patrician houses on one intriguing street after another. Stroll through the halls and colonnades of the Imperial Palace. Wander beside the stream which flows through the old town. Visit the museum with its models of medieval Goslar.

If you plan to return to Hameln or Hannover, you might enjoy a stop at Einbeck, another medieval town once famed for its six hundred breweries. Carvings touched with color brighten the wooden houses grouped around the Marktplatz. From Einbeck you can head north through the scenic Leine valley.

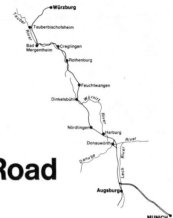

Medieval gems on the Romantic Road

These delightful old towns are for lingering

Romanticists with a passion for the past will find one of the most pleasant routes in Germany to be the *Romantische Strasse*. Wending its way north from the Austrian border to Würzburg, this "Romantic Road" leads you to delightful towns where time stands still.

High ramparts surround the towns, as they have for centuries. Once you drive through the thick city gates, you enter a medieval world of steeply-gabled buildings, cobblestone streets and ornate fountains.

This is a route for lingering and dreaming. Wander down appealing cobbled streets and stroll atop the medieval walls. Stop for a picnic beneath a roadside apple tree and watch farm families working in the fields. Dine or spend the night in a comfortable gabled inn.

The towns along this route escaped destruction during the Thirty Years' War (1618-1648), when much of Germany was devastated. Each summer Rothenburg and Dinkelsbühl re-enact the circumstances under which their towns were spared.

Walled towns

You leave Munich headed west on the Augsburg autobahn, and near that city, turn north to join the Romantic Road. Cross the Danube at Donauwörth, at its confluence with the Wörnitz River.

Donauwörth, situated on a hillside which descends to the Danube, is dominated by its Holy Cross Church. Old town walls still follow the banks of the Wörnitz, and the wide imperial road runs through the center of town.

The massive fortress of Harburg Castle looms protectively above its town, overlooking the Wörnitz valley. Stop by to explore the castle and the separate museum housing the castle's art treasures.

Approaching Nördlingen, you'll spot a majestic 300-foot-high church tower above the red roofs. Nördlingen's other striking asset is its remarkable perimeter wall, completely encircling the town. Try to linger here for a walk along the wall, exploring the narrow cobbled streets and enjoying the town's splashing fountain and wrought iron signs.

As you drive through the valley, you'll pass tractors on the road and see tractor and horse-drawn carts in the fields. During haying and harvest times, whole families are hard at work.

Drowsing Dinkelsbühl preserves its share of medieval fortifications. The quiet waters of the reed-bordered moat reflect its walls and watchtowers and gates. Inside the walls, tall gabled buildings brightened by blooming flowers face the main square. In summer you can climb to the top of the church tower for a view over the rooftops and walls. At dawn on Wednesdays you may wake to the sounds of cart wheels on the cobblestones and the grunting and squealing of pigs, signaling the gathering of farmers in Dinkelsbühl's market square for the weekly pig market.

Feuchtwangen is proud of its Roman cloisters. The local museum in a 17th-century peasant's house includes Franconian country furniture, costumes, and crafts.

Wrought-iron shop signs add a whimsical touch on a stroll through the delightful 16th-century town of Rothenburg.

At Donauwörth, the Romantic Road crosses the still-shallow Danube (top). Rothenburg's tile roofs rise above the Tauber valley (left). A city wall, cut by helmet-roofed towers, encircles Nördlingen (center). Gabled buildings face Dinkelsbühl's square (right).

Captivating Rothenburg

Rothenburg ob der Tauber, the favorite stopping place along the route, rises on a high promontory overlooking the Tauber valley. Visitors entering the narrow arch of a fortified gateway are immediately plunged into the Middle Ages. The atmosphere of a 16th-century town surrounds you; within the city ramparts you walk on cobbled streets, beneath arched towers, past tall gabled buildings with steeply-pitched roofs. Ornate wrought iron signs announce the shops, flowers bloom in window boxes, water splashes in old stone fountains. Each street and alley invites you to explore.

Rothenburg managed to escape destruction during the Thirty Years' War, but the depression which followed left the town too poor to build and expand. The town has also been spared in subsequent wars and is now officially preserved as a typical 16th-century town.

Facing the Marktplatz is the imposing town hall. Built during different periods, its architecture combines Gothic and Renaissance. If you're feeling energetic, you can climb to the top of the belfry for a view over the town. On the north side of the square, the clock in the gable of the Ratstrinkstube tavern has carved characters which enact the town's wine legend daily at 11 A.M., noon, 1, 2 and 3 P.M. Gabled mansions built by prosperous burghers line the Herrngasse, off the Marktplatz.

Be sure to allow time for a leisurely walk along the ramparts which surround the town. Many of the towers have stairs leading to the wall-top walkway. A public garden on the western promontory overlooks the wooded Tauber valley; far below, a two-tiered bridge crosses the river. In summer you can sometimes arrange for a ride in a horse-drawn carriage into the valley and to the nearby village of Detwang.

The spires of St. Jakob-Kirche mark Rothenburg's foremost art treasure: a striking altarpiece depicting the Last Supper, the work of master carver Tilman Riemenschneider. His work is found elsewhere in the Tauber valley, particularly in the little church in Detwang and in the isolated Herrgottskirche near Creglingen (take the Blaufelden road).

Two historic festivals

Festivals in Dinkelsbühl and Rothenburg re-enact how the towns were spared during the Thirty Years' War.

Rothenburg was taken by the imperial commander Tilly in 1631. Pleas for mercy failed until, on a whim, he offered to spare the town if a leading citizen could empty in one drink a tankard containing 3½ quarts of wine. Burgomaster Nusch rose to the occasion by manfully quaffing the spirits and saving the town. Costumed residents perform the *Meistertrunk* (Master Drink) play on Whit Sunday and Monday; on Whit Monday afternoon, the town residents parade through the streets in medieval dress, then celebrate with a giant town picnic.

Dinkelsbühl was spared by invaders who deferred to the pleas of the town's children. The annual "Kinderzeche" festival takes place on the third Monday in July; it includes the historic play and a parade of the Dinkelsbühl boys' band in period costumes.

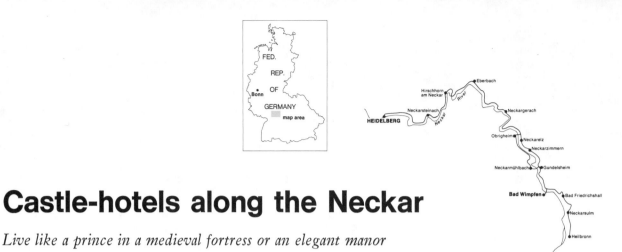

Castle-hotels along the Neckar

Live like a prince in a medieval fortress or an elegant manor

In the 50 miles between Heidelberg and Heilbronn, the meandering waters of the Neckar River mirror a delightful succession of castles, vineyards, and villages. Excursion boats cruise upriver from Heidelberg to Neckarsteinach from April to September.

A dozen castles of varying shapes and sizes crown the high crags or nestle in the valley. Some are in ruins; others are still occupied by aristocratic families. But six ancient strongholds and manor houses have been converted to castle-hotels where you can stay a night or two and soak up some of the glory of the distant past.

If the idea of living in a castle appeals to you, write to the German National Tourist Office for their detailed brochure (see page 75).

Germany's castle-hotels

Sleeping in a castle-hotel can give a new dimension to foreign travel. These noble shelters differ greatly in terms of size, age, original purpose, and state of repair. Properly, a fortified castle built as a defensive stronghold is called a *Burg* in Germany; a residential castle or manor house is a *Schloss*.

These terms overlap, as did the purpose of the original castles, but usually a *Schloss-hotel* is a great house with a history of continuous occupation, while a snug *Burg-hotel* is enclosed or flanked by mossy ruined walls and towers perhaps a thousand years old.

As interest in the castle-hotels has grown, new ones have been added to the ever-increasing list. Proprietors have remodeled dungeons into kitchens and intimate taverns, or walled redoubts have been transformed into open-air terrace cafes.

Bedrooms in the converted castles range from candle-lit chambers to luxurious suites. Some rooms have private baths, but usually you'll have to walk down the hall. Your castle-hotel may feature a lounge with a large open fireplace, a spiral staircase, or its own garden-park or private vineyard.

Overnight along the Neckar

On the castle-studded drive between Heidelberg and Heilbronn, you can choose from among six castle-hotels along the Neckar.

Burg Hirschhorn, the first one upriver from Heidelberg, still seems to stand guard over the walled village below. The watchtower and turreted walls of the present castle were built in the 12th century and later enlarged, so you see walls beyond walls and, inside the present town, the remains of a deep moat. The Renaissance castle makes a spacious, brightly-windowed inn—a fine base for exploring the rambling castle ruins, nearby

From tower of Hornberg Castle you look down on enclosed courtyard, terraced vineyards, and Neckar River at right.

Hirschhorn Castle stands protectively on a wooded spur above its walled village (right); you stay in the light-toned building at the right of the upper tower. The thick walls of Schloss Lehen are exposed at a wall niche in the dining room of this castle-hotel (left).

wooded paths, and village. Meals are served in pleasant dining rooms or on the outdoor terrace overlooking the hills, village, and busy Neckar.

Two castle-hotels on the left bank of the river can be reached by crossing the Neckar at Diedesheim to Obrigheim, then driving upstream.

Schloss Neuberg sits high above the river. The oldest part of the castle—the cellars, ground floor, and Knights' Hall—dates back about a thousand years. Meals are served in a cozy restaurant or on a terrace with a fine view. You can go for walks in the nearby forest.

Schloss Hochhausen, about 2½ miles upstream from Obrigheim, was originally a palace during the early Middle Ages, then remodeled in 1752 to late baroque style. All the rooms are furnished in period furniture. You can relax in the lounge in front of the open fireplace or walk in the large garden-park with its old trees.

Upriver from Neckarelz, near the village of Neckarzimmern, the stark ruins of Burghotel Hornberg jut into the sky above its own steep, terraced vineyards. This romantic-looking fortress dating from 1040 is the oldest of the Neckar castles, although the guest rooms have been recently remodeled and modernized. You'll stay in buildings facing the small courtyard below the castle towers. The former stable is now a combination dining room, bar, and general gathering-place. Windows in the dining room offer a panorama over the castle vineyards, the village of Neckarzimmern, and the valley of the Neckar River.

Two luxurious Neckar castle-hotels near the resort towns of Bad Wimpfen and Bad Friedrichshall stand in the center of their own garden-parks.

Schloss Heinsheim accommodates guests in a baroque-style manor and neighboring guest house. You might see a festive wedding party here, for the building has its own palace chapel. Estate gardens provide home-grown produce, and wines come from the castle's private vineyard.

Compact, thick-walled Schloss Lehen can be found at the edge of Bad Friedrichshall, near enough to stroll into town if you like. Built during the 1400s, the castle is both cozy and elegant, and redolent with atmosphere and niceties of service. In summer, umbrella-shaded tables brighten the front lawn.

Riverside diversions

The drive between Heidelberg and Heilbronn takes several hours, but diversions along the way can easily prolong your trip.

In addition to the castle-hotels, three other castles are of interest. Zwingenberg Castle, south of Eberbach, sits atop a promontory. Here you can see unusual wall paintings in the chapel. Guttenberg Castle at Neckarmühlbach, 12½ miles north of Heilbronn, is one of the oldest and best preserved of the Neckar castles. The Neckarsulm Palace of the Teutonic Order houses the German Bicycle Museum.

You'll find Bad Wimpfen a town of considerable charm. Its upper town, looking down on the Neckar, has a network of delightful streets lined with half-timbered houses. The gateway and several towers date from the medieval fortified town, the 13th-century imperial residence of the Hohenstaufen family. Salt brought prosperity to this entire region, and you can see the Ludwigshalle Saltworks along the base of the hill.

Bavaria's Alpine vacationland

Royal castles and attractive mountain villages await you

Eccentric Ludwig II, who sprinkled castles through the Bavarian Alps, anticipated popular interest in this area by nearly a century when he located his architectural fantasies here. For his mountain kingdom has now become Germany's southern playground. Here snowy peaks jut abruptly skyward, forming a majestic backdrop to mountain lakes and chalet villages. South of Munich you can visit splendid castles and a beautiful church, linger in Bavarian resorts, walk mountain paths, and ascend by cog railway or aerial tram to the top of Germany's highest peak.

Mountain resorts are at their busiest during the winter, when enthusiasts flock to fashionable Garmisch—site of the 1936 Winter Olympics—and smaller towns for skiing, skating, and other winter sports.

In summer the Alpine towns attract hikers and mountaineers. Other visitors seek out the small lakes scattered through the region. Your hotel may be a large Bavarian

chalet with overhanging roof, wooden balcony, and window boxes brimming with bright red geraniums.

Often you will see Bavarians in peasant costumes, women dressed in colorful dirndls, men in short leather breeches, fancy suspenders, and a Tyrolean hat.

Visiting the royal castles

As you drive south through the Lech valley toward the old mountain town of Füssen, the greyish white towers of Neuschwanstein Castle thrust skyward above dark green pines. Beyond, the spurs of the Alps provide a magnificent backdrop. A side road leads east to the royal castles of Hohenschwangau and Neuschwanstein.

Hohenschwangau was the country retreat of the Bavarian royal family when they wanted to escape court life in Munich. Its walls and ceilings are elaborately decorated, many murals portraying medieval heroes. Notorious Ludwig II, who became king at the age of 19 in 1864, was an admirer and patron of Richard Wagner, and the composer visited Hohenschwangau many times. In the music room on the second floor you'll see mementoes of their long association.

Ludwig's mania for building extravagant castles depleted the royal treasury and ultimately caused him to be deposed in 1886. From his bedroom window at Hohenschwangau, he could watch through a telescope the building process at Neuschwanstein.

As you walk up the long approach road, you begin to appreciate the difficulty of such a massive construction project on this isolated site. (Tired sightseers can arrange to ride up the hill in a horse-drawn cart.)

Feudal-style Neuschwanstein, with its turrets and pinnacles, evokes a dreamlike atmosphere. Inside you find rooms decorated with marble, gilded paneling, heavy tapestries, magnificent chandeliers and candelabras. You'll see Ludwig's artificial grotto, the unfinished throne room, the great Singer's Hall, and the castle kitchens.

Another of Ludwig's castles was Linderhof, a small palace deep in a forested valley west of Oberammergau. Although used primarily as a hunting lodge, Linderhof was built to resemble an Italian villa. Its interior is opulently decorated, and it is surrounded by a park with

In Mittenwald, *known for its violinmaking tradition, you'll see painted houses and balconied Bavarian chalets.*

White towers of storybook Neuschwanstein Castle rise in a spectacular setting (left). You can walk from nearby Hohenschwangau Castle. Zugspitze cable car rises above the clouds into full sunlight (center). Linderhof Castle (right) was used as a royal hunting lodge.

formal gardens, fountains, and pools. Don't miss the Moorish pavilion and grotto that Ludwig used whenever he decided to play Oriental ruler.

The Bavarian Alps

Your only regret on a visit to this Alpine vacationland may be that you don't have more time to spend there. All around are flowery Alps to be trod and snowy peaks to be climbed. A profusion of chair lifts and aerial tramways provide access to the highest points.

At Garmisch-Partenkirchen, one of the world's top winter sports centers, the Olympic skiing and skating facilities attract a fashionable crowd. In summer, life is quieter. Days are usually spent outdoors—in the mountains, by the lakes, or strolling around the twin towns.

Mittenwald nestles in a valley near the Austrian border, protected by the rocky wall of the Karwendel. Numerous colored houses brighten the town, many painted with historical or Biblical scenes. Skilled craftsmen have made stringed instruments here for nearly three hundred years, and a museum shows the evolution of the craft.

Attractive Oberammergau is known both for fine woodcarving and for its Passion Play, presented every ten years (next in 1980). A Biblical atmosphere pervades the town, many façades displaying murals with Biblical scenes and streets bearing names from the Bible. The Passion Play originated in the 1630s when, after the town was spared from a terrible plague, the people of the village vowed to present a play once each decade depicting the Passion of Christ. All of the 1,200 participants come from the town. More than a half million spectators witnessed the all-day performances in 1970.

Northwest of Oberammergau, off the main roads, you'll find the exuberantly-adorned church of Wies. Set in the meadows with a forest backdrop, it is considered by connoisseurs as the most beautiful rococo church in Germany.

Up Germany's highest peak

If time limits you to a single mountain goal, it may as well be the highest one around—the 9,731-foot Zugspitze, Germany's highest point. Its spectacular panorama, often called the finest in Europe, takes in the Bavarian and some of the Austrian, Swiss, and Italian Alps, as well as the hazy Swabian-Bavarian plateau of forests, meadows, lakes, and towns. A large deck offers sunbathers a quick tan in the clear, thin air, and you can watch skiers on the slopes below. If the weather turns windy or cold, you can escape to the glass-enclosed restaurant.

If you are not an accomplished mountaineer, you can make the ascent in two ways: by narrow-gauge cog railway or aerial tram. If you like, go up one way and come down the other.

The train trip takes about an hour from Garmisch. The railway meanders through pastoral countryside to the Eibsee, then steepens as the train heads inside the mountain, climbing smoothly in a winding 3-mile tunnel that ends near the Schneefernerhaus. A short aerial tram continues on to the upper cable station.

The gigantic aerial tramway makes a 10-minute cable trip from the Eibsee, climbing 6,000 feet up the sheer north face of the mountain.

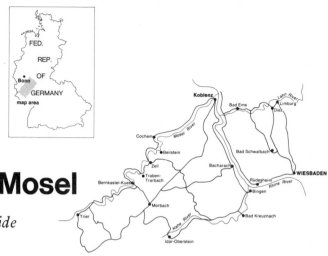

Wine tasting along the Mosel

Leisurely exploring in the quiet German countryside

Wine fanciers will be at their mellow best during the autumn grape harvest in Germany's wine country. There's special pleasure in sampling the local wine while workers gather the current year's grapes in the nearby vineyards, and wine towns are most festive at harvest time. But you will enjoy this peaceful, relaxing region in other seasons as well.

The winding valley of the Mosel (called Moselle in France, where it originates) lends itself particularly well to leisurely exploring. Diversions are simple—pleasant towns, hillside vineyards, towering castles, marvelous wines. Several castle hotels near the Mosel accommodate overnight guests (see page 75). Or perhaps a local inn or pension may be more to your liking. During summer and fall you'll probably need advance reservations.

Navigable for nearly 170 miles, the Mosel is a river highway busy with barges transporting freight. From late May to mid-October excursion boats make the trip daily between Koblenz and Cochem, Cochem and Bernkastel, Bernkastel and Trier.

The heart of the Mosel wine country begins south of Cochem and continues intermittently all the way to Trier. You follow along the winding river, crossing from one bank to the other. Almost every town is a wine-making center, its steeply-terraced vineyards facing south to catch the full warmth of the sun.

German wineries seldom invite the public to visit the winery and sample the wares. If you make your own private, advance arrangements, you may get inside a winery. But the best place to savor the region's wines is in one of the local hotels that has a robust wine list or in a friendly *Weinstube*.

Up the Mosel from Koblenz

Boat excursions on both the Mosel and Rhine leave from Koblenz, at the confluence of the rivers. If you're here overnight, stop in to enjoy the open-air music and wine gardens in the Weindorf, along the Rhine just upriver from the main bridge.

As you drive up the broad, green Mosel valley, castles and ruined fortresses tower over riverside villages. The most scenic stretch begins near Cochem, where the valley becomes steeper, the foliage more abundant, the river more twisting. From Cochem you can walk up to the castle through the vineyards, taking the Schloss-Strasse up from the Markt.

You cross by car ferry to Beilstein, clustered below its large church and castle. You'll enjoy exploring these small wine villages; roads and footpaths lead to castle ruins and into the hills.

The town of Bernkastel-Kues spans the Mosel. You

Splendid castle crowns the vineyard-covered hill above Cochem; you can walk up to the castle from the town.

Decorated hotel at Bernkastel-Kues
is typical of the small inns
you'll find along the winding Mosel (left).
Beilstein is tucked into a deep bend
of the river; a small ferry makes
frequent trips across the Mosel (right).

can taste the fruity Bernkastel vintages in local cellars. And in early September the town celebrates the new harvest with one of the major Mosel wine festivals.

Trier, one of Germany's oldest cities, was founded by the Romans in the 1st century B.C. The huge Porta Nigra fortress is Trier's landmark. Relics of the Roman era are displayed in the Rhineland Museum; the ruins of the Imperial Baths can also be visited. Markets have been held in the Hauptmarkt for over a thousand years. From Trier it is only a short drive to Luxembourg and France.

If you want to return to Koblenz, a fast high road skims the top of the Hunsrück ridge east of the river. Or take one of the less heavily traveled back roads through arching woods and quiet farmland.

More nearby excursions

If journeying along the Mosel has whetted your appetite for more of the German countryside, sample the wine country along the Rhine or Nahe valleys, or head north to the heavily wooded mountains of the Taunus.

A favorite boat excursion cruises through the Rhine gorge from Koblenz upstream to Rüdesheim; motorists have a choice of scenic roads along both river banks. Castles and ruins crown the high points, vineyards climb the hills, barges chug along the river, and one attractive town after another tempts you to stop. Here, too, you'll find friendly inns and a few castle hotels.

Another possibility is the drive east from Morbach to the quiet route along the Nahe River. The Nahe vineyards are centered around Bad Kreuznach, and Nahe wines are more mellow than the Mosel wines.

North of the Rhine, the twisting Lahn River separates the densely-wooded mountains of the Westerwald and the Taunus. Ruined castles cling to the hillsides, and small towns nestle in the river bends. Why not pick up supplies for a picnic, either along the river or in the sun-dappled beech forests of the Taunus?

PICNICKING POINTERS

Picnicking provides a delightful midday break, a pause from travel or sightseeing when you relax outdoors in the fresh air. Roadside picnicking is commonplace in Europe, particularly along secondary and rural roads. But you can also plan to picnic in the city park.

Shopping for your food is part of the fun. In most towns you must seek out several stores to assemble your picnic supplies. You'll find meats and cheeses in one shop, bread at the bakery, bottles of wine in the wine shop, cookies and pastries in the pastry shop, fresh fruit at the grocery or in the open-air market. You pick and choose and point, dealing with friendly clerks who seldom meet foreign travelers.

If you prefer, perhaps your hotel will prepare a picnic lunch if you request it the night before.

Plan to bring minimum picnic supplies from home: nested plastic glasses, corkscrew or bottle operer, a sharp knife, individual chemically-treated paper towels. Depending on your picnicking style, consider a small cutting board, miniature salt and pepper shakers, a small picnic cloth and napkins, can opener, nested paper plates, silverware. You'll want a net or string bag to carry your purchases.

Finding a spot can be as simple as pulling off the road beneath a tree or sitting in a grassy unfenced field. Perhaps you'll find a pleasant site beside a river or stream. Good manners demand that you avoid trespassing and that you carry away your trash.

In the city, spread out your picnic on a park bench, or head for greenery along a nearby river or lake. Perhaps your hotel concierge can suggest a pleasant site only a short bus ride from the center of town.

Picnicking allows you to relax in a pastoral setting, savoring food experiences different from those found in restaurants or hotel dining rooms. In addition to being fun, it's the perfect answer for travelers who prefer to avoid a heavy midday meal. You can cut food expenses, perhaps allowing for a special splurge at dinner time.

Into the Black Forest

Folk traditions and forest paths are special charms

Though the name Black Forest may sound foreboding, in reality the area is no more sinister than the cuckoo clocks it produces. For one thing, it is not really black. Nor is it a forest in the true sense. Dark evergreens cover the slopes of smoothly rounded mountains, giving the region its name, but the valleys are green with open fields.

Nestled in the elbow of the Rhine River and extending north to Karlsruhe, the Black Forest stretches for more than a hundred miles in Germany's southwestern corner. This year-round holiday area appeals to persons who enjoy bracing air and mountain scenery. An added attraction is the charm of folk traditions and costumes which have been preserved. Driving through the mountain valleys, you'll often see the *Schwarzwaldhaus*, the huge wooden farmhouse characteristic of the region,

sheltering people and animals under one roof. Stables are at ground level, living quarters above, and barn and workshop on the top.

Folk costumes are worn most often on Sundays, church holidays, and at local festivals. Most famous is the one from the Gutach valley, where women wear the immense *Bollenhut* (see photo). Married women wear hats with black pompons; young girls wear red ones. These may sometimes still be seen in Kirnbach near Wolfach and in Reichenbach near Hornberg.

Forest roads and towns

Three north-south scenic routes link Baden-Baden with Freudenstadt: the Baden Wine Road follows the wine villages of the western foothills; the Black Forest High Road cuts south through forest and mountain landscape; the Black Forest Low Road follows the Murg Valley through Gernsbach and Forbach.

No single route dominates the country south of Freudenstadt, although main roads follow the valleys of the Kinzig and Gutach rivers. You'll pass small wayside towns—some quietly drowsing, others busy with the local watch and cuckoo clock industry. Expect many forest roads to be narrow and winding and main routes often to be crowded. Allow a full half day for driving between Freudenstadt and Freiburg.

Along the way are numerous roadside viewpoints, and forest car parks have marked trails leading into the woods (see page 75). Walkers and hikers roam countless miles of well-marked and maintained trails through beautiful woodlands, across lush meadows, up winding ridges or down wild gorges.

Triberg's local museum is devoted to Black Forest traditions, local costumes, and regional crafts. You might also enjoy following the path from Triberg up the shaded ravine to see 531-foot Gutach Falls.

At Furtwangen, the center of the watch and clock industry, a collection of historic clocks is on display. West of Furtwangen, up the Katzensteig valley, you can visit the source of the Danube at Donauquelle, where the river begins its 1800-mile journey to the Black Sea.

Traditional costumes are often seen at festivals; women of the Gutach valley wear a headdress with huge pompons.

IN GERMANY: special interests

SPECIALIZED MUSEUMS • Germany offers a number of museums devoted to a special subject; some of these may pique your interest. Along the Rhine, the Museum of Cutlery at Solingen explains how an old handicraft developed into a modern industry; the World Museum of Printing in Mainz shows the history of printing; and the Wine Museum in Speyer portrays the role of wine through the centuries.

In the Black Forest you can visit the Jewelry Museum at Pforzheim or view the collection of clocks and watches at Furtwangen. The Daimler-Benz Museum in Stuttgart-Untertürkheim contains old and new models of motor cars and some Mercedes racing cars.

Along Lake Constance you'll find the Open-Air Museum of German Prehistory in Unteruhldingen, with its reconstructed village of pile dwellings; the Doll and Doll House Museum at Frauenberg Castle near Bodman; and the Zeppelin Museum, showing the construction of dirigible aircraft, in Friedrichshafen.

You can visit a Museum of Violinmaking in Mittenwald in the Bavarian Alps; a Hat Museum in Bad Homburg near Frankfurt, showing four centuries of changing headgear styles; a Leather Museum at Offenbach on the Main, also near Frankfurt; and the German Bread Museum in Ulm on the Danube.

CAMPING IN GERMANY • More than 1700 camping areas await outdoorsmen in the Federal Republic of Germany. You'll find areas near the sea, in the mountains, nestled in peaceful valleys and wooded hills, near rivers and lakes, bordering medieval towns. Some are convenient for an overnight stopover; others are ideal for a longer stay.

The German National Tourist Office issues a marked map brochure noting the locations of more than 400 camping areas. Detailed campground information is compiled in annual guidebooks issued by the DCC (German Camping Club) and the German ADAC (Automobile Club).

CALENDAR OF EVENTS • Twice a year the German National Tourist Office issues a folder listing coming events in Germany. Included are exhibitions and fairs, major art shows, theater and music events, historical plays, religious events, folk festivals and old customs, sporting events, conventions and congresses, special events and anniversary celebrations.

HIKING TRAILS FOR MOTORISTS • Travelers who wish to break their drive with a short walk in the woods will find car parks for hikers in scenic regions throughout Germany. Well-marked circular footpaths, beginning and ending at the parking area, have been laid out for the convenience of motorists.

Car parks with circular hiking paths are marked with a blue sign displaying a white capital P and the figures of two hikers. At the parking area a large sign is marked with the various routes, length of each trail in kilometers, main sights, and average time required. Most of the trails are two to five miles long, although some are longer. Nature paths (*Naturlehrpfade*) have signs along the way (in German).

OKTOBERFEST • Munich is swimming in cheer—and beer—during its great fall festival that gets underway in mid-September. For two weeks beer flows freely in a holiday atmosphere. Villagers from all over Bavaria, many of them in peasant costumes or loden suits, gather in the city. Colorful banners and streamers enliven the streets. The festival begins the third Saturday of September when the horse-drawn beer wagons arrive and the mayor taps the first keg. On Sunday comes the great parade of national costumes, marksmen's clubs, flower-decorated beer wagons, bands, and colorful floats. Huge beer tents and a carnival are set up on the festival grounds. During the following two weeks a million gallons of beer are consumed while Bavarian oompah bands play well into the night.

TRAVEL TO WEST BERLIN • You can reach West Berlin from the Federal Republic by plane, train, bus, or car. Travelers arriving by air need only a valid passport. For trips by train, bus, or automobile, however, a transit visa through the German Democratic Republic (East Germany) is required in addition to a passport. The visa is issued on board the trains and for cars at the border checkpoints: Helmstedt/Marienborn, Rudolphstein/Hirschberg; Herleshausen/Wartha-Leipzig; and Lauenburg/Horst. You can also enter East Germany from Scandinavia and Austria. Obtain a visa for your return trip at the same time you get the entry visa.

CASTLE HOTELS • If you've always wanted to live in a castle, write to the German National Tourist Office for information about castles that have been converted into hotels. Many historic fortresses and mansions offer accommodations for overnight guests.

CHRISTMAS MARKETS • The Christmas holiday season is a particularly joyous time in Germany. Stalls of the Christmas markets, stocked with toys, ornaments and holiday decorations, open early in December. Nürnberg has the largest and finest of the Christmas fairs (*Christkindlmarkt*). Other German cities holding holiday markets include Hannover, Munich, Rothenburg ob der Tauber, and West Berlin.

HOBBY VACATIONS • If you would like to spend part of your time in Germany developing or improving a skill or hobby, the range of activities is wide. You can spend a week hiking, mountain climbing, golfing, playing tennis, horseback riding, ice skating, or skiing. If you have linguistic leanings, take a short course in German language instruction. For more information on hobby vacations, see your travel agent or write the German National Tourist Office.

German National Tourist Offices
630 Fifth Avenue, New York, N.Y. 10020
104 S. Michigan Avenue, Chicago, Ill. 60603
700 S. Flower Street, Los Angeles, Calif. 90017

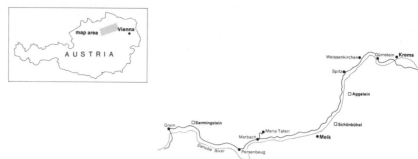

Along the peaceful Danube

Follow the route of the Romans, the Crusaders, and Napoleon

Whether you travel Austria's Danube Valley by automobile, local bus or train, or passenger boat, a potpourri of sights awaits you. Between Grein and Krems, forested hills give way to cultivated fields, fruit orchards, and terraced vineyards. You'll see ancient castles and imposing abbeys punctuating the sky, and along the river you'll discover quiet villages that invite you to linger and explore. Now and then you'll pass an inviting *Gasthaus* (inn) ready to offer simple food and local wine, along with a close-up view of the river and its traffic.

Throughout the centuries, the Danube Valley has been a strategic route—or barrier—between Europe and the East. The Romans, Huns, and Crusaders passed along this grey-brown river highway; later came the Turks, followed by the Swedes during the Thirty Years' War; after them came Napoleon. Local rulers built castles on the narrow crags high above the river. Along its banks, they constructed fortified villages to collect taxes from passing ships carrying salt, iron, and wine.

Along the north bank of the river, a scenic highway winds between the water and the hills. Ferries cross the Danube near Grein, Marbach, Melk, Spitz, and Weissenkirchen. From May to September, boats cruise regularly between Passau and Vienna and from Vienna to the Wachau region.

Downstream from Grein

Set below its château, the attractive country resort of Grein lies at the foot of a wooded bluff. You can reach the castle by trail. The road to the east heads into the deep ravine of the Strudengau, past the ruins of Struden Castle and the castle of Sarmingstein. The Danube widens into a lake behind the Ybbs-Persenbeug dam.

Beyond Persenbeug, you enter the region known as the Nibelungengau; in the 4th and 5th centuries this was the home of the Nibelung tribe, whose legends were dramatized in opera by Richard Wagner.

The magnificent Abbey of Melk, its dome and symmetrical towers standing out against the sky, overlooks the Danube from a high bluff on the south bank. To reach it, take the car ferry across the river. One of the most beautiful of Austria's existing baroque churches, it also has a vivid history.

First built as a castle in the 10th century, the building was turned over to the Benedictine order and converted into a fortified abbey. The monastery was gutted by fire during the Turkish invasion of 1683. After it was rebuilt in the 18th century, Napoleon established his headquarters here in 1805 and 1809 during his successful campaigns against Austria.

You can visit the Abbey daily (closed noon to 2 P.M.)

Terraced vineyards drop toward the river near Krems. A scenic highway follows the valley's north side.

Ruined fortress of Aggstein (top left) and Maria Taferl abbey (bottom left) stand as sentinels above the Danube valley. At the eastern end of the Wachau is Krems, entered through its massive Steiner Tor (right).

to see some of the many artistic treasures preserved within the immense complex of buildings. Dominating the monastery is the beautiful church, lavishly decorated in the baroque style.

Through the Wachau

East of Melk you enter the part of the valley known as the Wachau, with its vineyards, riverside villages, and impressive castle ruins.

The best way to enjoy the Wachau is to stay in a Danube-side village for several days and explore the area in a leisurely fashion. In spring, fruit trees blossom; in summer, wildflowers add their colorful accent; in September and October, clusters of grapes hang heavy on the vines, and vintners' villages celebrate the harvest with local festivities.

Many of these riverside towns were founded in the 9th and 10th centuries. Almost every one has its quiet square and old houses, dominated by a beautiful Gothic church. Many of the churches contain beautiful paintings or carved wooden statues.

Vineyard villages

Downstream from Melk on the right bank, the ruins of Aggstein mark the site of one of the most formidable fortresses in the Wachau. You can reach it by a steep footpath from the village.

Small villages dot the northern side of the Danube between Melk and Krems. Spitz lies off the road, hidden behind fruit trees and vineyards; a short detour leads to the town with its old houses, arcades, and 15th-century parish church. Downstream is the fortified church of St. Michael, flanked by a round tower.

In the charming medieval market town of Weissenkirchen, a covered wooden stairway leads up to the fortified parish church. Villagers surrounded it with a wall in the 16th century to protect it from invading Turks.

Dürnstein is one of the prettiest of the Wachau wine villages, with the ruins of Dürnstein Castle towering above it. According to legend, King Richard the Lion-Hearted was imprisoned here in 1193 while returning from the Crusades. A rocky path leads to the ruins.

Walls were built up from the river to surround the village. Inside the gate, medieval and Renaissance houses and inns line the narrow streets. Just off the main street is the village church, known throughout Austria for its baroque architecture and stucco ceiling.

Krems and the neighboring town of Stein mark the eastern end of the Wachau. Famous for its vineyards, Krems has a wine museum showing items connected with the vineyards of the Danube valley.

AUSTRIA 77

South from Salzburg

A splendid sampling of Austria's attractions

In Austria's delightful Salzkammergut, cozy towns and villages snuggle along curving lakeshores and mountain valleys; subterranean pathways penetrate ancient salt mines and ice caves; cable cars and cog railways climb to mountaintop lookouts. Some thirty lakes nestle amid the green valleys, wooded hills, and towering peaks.

Because salt mining has played an important role here since prehistoric days, the syllable *salz* or *hall* (both meaning "salt") is a part of many place names in the Salzburg region. Salt mines are still worked, and several are open to adventurous travelers (see page 85).

Be forewarned: during warm weather it rains often in the lake district. In sunny autumn, there's a nip in the air; many rural towns mark the harvest season with noisy, joyous festivals.

Up the Salzach Valley

From Salzburg's old town on the river's left bank, drive south up the gentle Salzach Valley toward the mountains.

Ancient Hallein grew up around its salt mining and refining industry. Today the Dürnberg mines, reached by cable car, are a favorite day excursion for Salzburg visitors from May through October.

Wooded hills enclose the Tennengau basin above Hallein. From the village of Golling, a short detour leads to the Golling waterfalls. Cross the Salzach bridge, following *Wasserfall* signs along country roads.

South of Golling, drive east along the Lammer River gorge to the pastoral Abtenau basin. Here tiny belfries cap the chalet farmhouses, and field fences of interwoven laths border the roads. Summer and fall travelers see hay drying on long racks.

Once you've descended the steep eastern flank of Gschütt Pass to the village of Gosau, take a side road about four miles south to Lake Gosau and its breathtaking view. The mirror-like waters of this unspoiled alpine lake reflect the high, rugged peaks of the Dachstein and its icy glaciers. In early morning or late afternoon, as light bathes the peaks and glaciers while the valley floor is in shadow, your view is especially memorable. Footpaths lead around the lake and up the valley.

Austria's oldest community

Hallstatt's balconied houses cling precariously to a wooded slope above the deep blue waters of Lake Hallstatt. Behind the town's steeply-pitched roofs rise the sheer granite walls of the Dachstein. Narrow, curving streets follow the contours of the steep hillside, into which Celtic tribes dug for salt a thousand years before Christ.

In the 19th century archaeologists discovered more than a thousand graves of these prehistoric lake dwellers, who built their homes on pilings above the lake waters. Because of these important discoveries, the early part of

Villagers and hikers *relax at a mountain cafe with a view of jagged Dachstein crags and alpine pastures.*

Dachstein ice caves (top) are reached by cable car that continues on to the Krippenstein summit (left). In salt mine tours in Hallein (bottom center) and Hallstatt, you wear coveralls and descend toboggan-style behind the guide. Hallstatt's roofs rise above the lake (right).

the Iron Age was named the "Hallstatt Period." Objects discovered during the excavations, including a miner's outfit from 2,500 years ago, are displayed in the museum.

Climb the steep covered stairway to the large parish church to see its handsome carved altar, then walk through Hallstatt's small cemetery. Lack of space makes it necessary to periodically dig up the bones, which are then placed in the small chapel at the rear of the graveyard.

If the water looks inviting, rent a rowboat or the long, flat-bottomed Hallstatt version of the gondola with its lofty prow (if you rent a gondola, you'd better arrange for a local boatman). Swimmers find pleasant beaches on the eastern shore near Obertraun. Summer evenings are usually warm enough for lingering over dinner in outdoor lakeside restaurants.

Ice caves and salt mines

From Obertraun a cable car takes you up the Dachstein to the famous ice caves, continuing to the summit of the Krippenstein, an impressive viewpoint overlooking the Dachstein plateau. Getting an early start in summer, you should plan at least a half day for the full trip and tour of the caves (open May to mid-October). Don't forget a warm wrap, for the temperature inside the caves stays near freezing even in midsummer.

Lights illuminate the subterranean caverns of the Giant's Ice Cave, hanging icicles and ice draperies creating a fairytale scene. In the nearby Mammoth's Cave, you follow the guide through a labyrinth of passages

into a majestic cavern over 130 feet high.

Hallstatt's salt mines (open May through September) are reached by the Salzberg cable railway. The mine entrance and museum are a short walk from the upper station.

Sampling the Salzkammergut

From the mid-19th century to the outbreak of World War I, Bad Ischl was the fashionable summer resort of Europe's royal families and leading personalities in the theater, music, and art world. From his villa in the landscaped Kaiserpark (open to visitors from Easter through October), Emperor Franz Josef presided over the lighthearted group as they waltzed to Johann Strauss melodies and hummed songs from Franz Lehar operettas.

One of the Salzkammergut's gems is the lake of St. Wolfgang. Sailboats flit across the water between Strobl at one end, St. Gilgen at the other, and St. Wolfgang on the northern shore. In keeping with the holiday atmosphere, you can travel by boat from the southern shore to St. Wolfgang. The town church, atop a rocky spur, is known for its artistic altar, but don't miss the arcaded cloisters high above the water where you catch glimpses of the lake. You'll also want to stroll along the shore to the Weisses Rössl, the famed White Horse Inn which once inspired an operetta.

From mid-May through September, an old-fashioned cogwheel train leaves St. Wolfgang to chug up the slopes of the Schafberg. On a clear day you can see from the summit more than a dozen of the Salzkammergut lakes.

Seeing Austria by local train

Travel is informal on the narrow-gauge railways

In this era of high-speed, direct-line travel, Europe's friendly narrow-gauge railroads have a special charm. Austria has preserved a number of these small railways, serving some of the country's most unspoiled regions. Some still use the original steam locomotives and coaches. Through the years, an affectionate relationship has grown between the people living along the rail lines and "their" railways.

The train often consists of an engine and just one or two cars. Since the conductor and engineer know many of the people along the line, service is personal. The train provides regular transportation both for women on their way to market and for energetic schoolboys bound for classrooms. You'll hear a cheery toot as the train passes waving children.

You can be the engineer

In Styria's Mur valley, railfans can fulfill the childhood dream of being the engineer on a steam locomotive. For a moderate fee, you can drive the engine yourself for part or all of the trip between Unzmarkt and Mauterndorf. You must make arrangements in advance for driving time, available in quarter-hour segments. A qualified engineer goes along as fireman; if necessary, he can give instructions for handling the engine.

Some narrow-gauge railways

Below are ten narrow-gauge railways in Austria, listed by province, that might fit into your itinerary. Additional information can be obtained from your travel agent or the Austrian National Tourist Office. Timetable numbers from the Official Timetable of the Austrian Federal Railways are included for your convenience in checking local schedules.

Lower Austria. St. Pölten to Mariazell (Styria) through the western Vienna woods to the pilgrimage city (timetable 11b).

Obergrafendorf to Wieselburg. Rural countryside south of the Danube River (timetable 11b).

Kienberg-Gaming to Lunz am See, a lakeside resort near the Styrian border (timetable 12a).

Lunz am See to Waidhofen an der Ybbs, through the beautiful Ybbs valley (timetable 12a).

Upper Austria. Garsten (near Steyr) to Molln along the Steyr River. The musical instrument known as the jew's harp is manufactured in Molln (timetable 13a).

Styria. Birkfeld to Weiz along the Feistritz River to a popular east Styrian resort (timetable 52c).

Unzmarkt to Mauterndorf (Salzburg) along the upper Mur valley via Murau; see item at left (timetable 63).

Salzburg. Zell am See to Krimml along the upper Salzach valley (timetable 23).

Tyrol. Mayrhofen to Jenbach down the Zillertal (timetable 31).

Jenbach to Achensee-Seespitz, up from the Inn Valley to a lovely mountain lake, from June through September (timetable 31a).

Amateur engineers can take the throttle on the Murtal Railway. People often wave as the train passes.

A day in the Vienna Woods

Wooded country roads lead you to charming wine villages

A magnet for Viennese families, the Vienna Woods draws them on weekends to hike its forest paths, savor local wines in the village *Heurigen* (wine gardens) or visit the region's towns and historic abbeys.

The thickly wooded, rolling hills of the *Wienerwald* stretch out from Vienna's suburbs to the north, west, and south. Country roads and hiking paths criss-cross the green hillsides and meadows, and quiet villages and towns nestle in the river valleys.

You'll discover plenty of picnic sites, or you may prefer to stop for lunch in a rustic, country *Gasthaus*.

Driving in the Wienerwald

Following the network of highways and country roads that spreads over the Vienna Woods and surrounding countryside, you'll find no shortage of attractive routes. Some of the road numbers have been changed recently, so use caution if you attempt to follow a map with route numbers.

A triangular loop to the southwest combines wooded back roads with some of the delightful wine villages south of Vienna. Head west from the capital along country roads and through small towns toward St. Pölten, then southeast past the site of the Mayerling tragedy. A side road leads to the Abbey of Heiligenkreuz. Renowned for its famous old spa waters, Baden is a favorite of many Viennese. You return to the capital through vineyards and wine towns that produce Austria's famous white wines. Vine-covered *Heurigen* in the wine villages of Gumpoldskirchen, Mödling, and Perchtoldsdorf give residents and visitors alike a pleasant opportunity to enjoy a mug of chilled wine.

Another route follows along the Danube, then swings back to let you return to Vienna through the woods. Drive north from the city to 12th-century Klosterneuburg Abbey, cutting through the woods to Tulln or continuing along the river past Greifenstein Castle.

Cross the river just as you enter Tulln and turn west toward Krems. Villages offer their backsides to the road, farmers preferring to decorate their inside courtyards in the East European manner. The road from Tulln through Neustift i. Felde and Grafenwörth passes a

Stop for lunch *in a country inn or* Heuriger, *where you can sample the local wine in a rustic atmosphere.*

huge field of flowers; during rose season you'll find a *Rosentankstelle* (rose service station), where you can buy a bunch of freshly-cut blooms.

You can break the trip with a stop at Schloss Grafenegg, a fascinating little castle enclosed by walls and a moat, just where the main road turns toward Krems. The castle grounds are planted with lovely gardens and abound in trees for children to climb and in spots for a picnic. The inside of the castle is open to visitors on summer weekends and holidays.

After visiting Krems, you can continue upriver to Dürnstein and Melk (see page 77) or cross the big bridge over the Danube and head south, past the monastery of Stift Göttweig, to St. Pölten, returning to Vienna by wooded back roads or autobahn. If you approach Vienna on the west autobahn, you can cut through the woods on the Wienerwald Autobahn southeast of Vienna to link up with the *Weinstrasse* and the wine villages.

In Burgenland, an inland sea

Near the Hungarian border is a vast nature preserve

One of Austria's most curious regions lies south of Vienna, where rolling hills give way to the great Central European plain, a country of wide horizons stretching eastward across Hungary.

Center of this district is Lake Neusiedl, the only "steppic" lake in Central Europe and the remains of a vast prehistoric sea that once covered the plain. In the thick band of reeds bordering the lake's shallow, salty waters —averaging only 3 feet in depth—more than 200 species of waterfowl make their home. Water sports enthusiasts sail, row, swim, and fish the lake from late spring to early fall. In winter the shallow lake freezes, becoming a vast arena for ice-sailing and skating.

Vineyards, fruit trees, and vegetables flourish in the mild climate and rich soil west and north of Lake Neusiedl. The vast expanse of the Hungarian *puszta* spreads eastward from the lake, with only an occasional windmill or well to relieve the flat landscape. Many visitors plan horseback trips across the puszta.

Burgenland was part of Hungary until 1918, and the frontier is not far away. In fact, the southern part of Lake Neusiedl lies in Hungarian territory. Don't plan to make a loop trip around the lake, however, as the Hungarian frontier cannot be crossed without a visa and border delays.

Nature preserves

From Vienna you drive southeast on the main Budapest route to Parndorf, turning south toward Lake Neusiedl.

If you're interested in ornithology, you'll want to visit the state biological station and lake museum at Neusiedl (open from Easter to November). Officials will show you bird photographs, and you'll learn about wildlife inhabiting the lakeshore marshes.

Vineyards appear south of Neusiedl, extending across the plain to Gols and beyond. As you approach the lake near Podersdorf, vines give way to orchards.

Families seek out the long sandy beach at Podersdorf, for even small children can play here without danger. This is the only spot along the lake where a wide fringe of reeds does not bar direct access to the lake. Swimming lasts from May to October. Sailboats and rowboats can be rented at lakeside piers, and in summer, motorboat trips link Neusiedl, Podersdorf, and Rust.

The lonely, rather desolate marshes of the Seewinkel region contain a collection of flora and fauna unsurpassed in Europe. Inquire in Illmitz or Wallern about guided excursions into this vast nature preserve. Approximately 200 kinds of waterfowl, including some of the continent's rarest species, nest in the marshland. The region shelters many small steppe animals as well, and unusual flowers bloom on the marshlands.

Villages of the puszta

East of Lake Neusiedl, the Hungarian puszta begins, a vast and level plain with patches of sparse, short grass

Riding on the puszta east of Lake Neusiedl is popular with visitors. Balance-hoist in rear marks a well.

Sailboats and rowboats break the horizon of Lake Neusiedl at sunset (left); you'll find boats for rent at lakeside piers. Storks return annually to nest on the chimneytops in Rust (center). Gypsy music provides part of the atmosphere in many of Burgenland's restaurants (right).

its only vegetation. Occasionally a windmill or well-head with balance-hoist breaks the monotony.

The villages in this steppe-like landscape have a distinctly Eastern character. Streets consist of rows of whitewashed one-story houses, each crowned with a pointed gable, some still roofed in reeds. Usually a porch leads to a large inner courtyard.

Many visitors enjoy a horseback ride across the puszta. Illmitz and Apetlon are riding centers; horses are also available in Podersdorf and Andau.

In the old settlements of St. Andrä and Frauenkirchen, villagers weave baskets using reeds gathered from nearby marshes. North of Halbturn, you'll see the baroque summer residence of Empress Maria Theresia, the Habsburg monarch who ruled the Austrian empire for forty years during the mid-18th century.

In this corner of Austria, you are seldom far from the Hungarian border. The village of Andau was a famous crossing point during the anti-Communist uprising in Hungary in 1956. From roads near the border, you can see the grim watchtowers and barbed wire fences.

Vineyards and storks

West of Lake Neusiedl, the lands present a different aspect. Overlooking the lake is a range of hills, fruit orchards, vineyards, corn, and garden vegetables growing in the rich soil at its base.

The wine villages of Rust, Oggau, and Mörbisch are strung out along the lake's western shore. Vineyards cover the plain and climb the terraced slopes. The small, sweet grapes have been grown in this district for over a thousand years.

Rust is also known for the storks that return each

spring to nest on chimney and rooftop platforms. From Rust and Mörbisch, roads lead across marshes and through the reeds to small swimming areas.

Mörbisch, last town on the western shore before the Hungarian frontier, is worth a stop. Narrow lanes and alleys lead off the main street at right angles, opening onto large courtyards. Many of the whitewashed houses have outdoor staircases, each surmounted by a porch. Shutters and doors are painted in bright colors, bunches of corn hang on exterior walls, and flowers add a bright touch to windows and balconies.

Near St. Margarethen you pass a giant quarry, the working site each summer for young sculptors. Their finished work remains here until sold, making the quarry a vast, open-air gallery.

Haydn's town

The spirit of composer Joseph Haydn lingers in Eisenstadt, located in the hills overlooking the plain. Eisenstadt, the capital of Burgenland, is an important wine market center. The region is at its most charming in spring when almond, apricot, and peach orchards bloom.

For thirty years, Haydn was a member of the court of Prince Esterhazy, whom he served as both composer and orchestra conductor. In Eisenstadt's great Esterhazy castle, you will see the Haydn room, the great hall decorated in frescoes where he conducted the court orchestra, often in his own compositions.

From Easter to late October you can visit his modest house at Haydngasse 21, where you'll see mementoes of his life and work. Follow the covered passageway to the flower-filled courtyard. Haydn's tomb, built of white marble, is in the local church.

Up the Ötztal to Obergurgl

Through the Tyrol to Austria's highest village

You probably won't arrive in Obergurgl by stratospheric balloon, as Auguste Piccard did one day in 1931, but the dramatic mountain road which winds up Austria's beautiful Ötz valley is an excellent alternative. You pass through a number of attractive Tyrolean mountain villages along the route to Obergurgl, tucked into a valley high in the sparkling clear air of the Tyrolean Alps — the highest village in Austria. Obergurgl's neighboring peaks and glaciers have made it a popular winter sports and summer mountaineering center.

It's a comfortable day trip to Obergurgl from Innsbruck. Head west up the Inn valley about 30 miles. Near Silz the road up the Ötztal branches south, rising in a series of natural steps to the alpine glaciers surrounding Obergurgl.

Tyrolean villages of the Ötztal

The road up the valley closely follows the cascading river and passes through a number of inviting small mountain villages, each with a sprinkling of Tyrolean chalets. First comes Ebene, with its covered bridge; then Ötz, a typical Tyrolean mountain community with painted façades and old parish church.

Peach and apricot orchards and corn fields, surprising in this region, owe their existence to the *Föhn* — the dry, hot wind which sweeps down alpine valleys north of the Alps.

You may want to stop at Umhausen, oldest community in the valley, to see the 17th-century room in the Gasthaus Krone or to walk to the nearby Stuiben waterfall.

Above Längenfeld the valley narrows to a gorge; below the road, the river crashes and foams among large boulders. Beyond Untergurgl the Timmelsjoch toll road branches off the main route, leading to the sports resort of Hochgurgl, the Timmelsjoch Pass, and an exceptionally scenic area of the Italian Alps near San Leonardo.

Excursions from Obergurgl

High in the mountains sits the tiny village of Obergurgl, surrounded by the ice-covered peaks of the Ötztaler Alps. A favorite mountaineering center, Obergurgl is the starting point for high alpine climbs and tours. Guides for tours across the glaciers to the high peaks can be hired in the village; a certified guide is necessary for extended excursions.

A two-section chairlift takes you from Obergurgl to the summit of the Hohe Mut spur for a panoramic view. In midsummer, after the snow has melted, walking and hiking trails let you penetrate deep into the Alps without pack gear. Such hikes, however, require stout boots and warm, windproof clothing.

Food and lodging are available at several Alpine Club houses within a three or four-hour hike from the village. If you plan to do much hiking, consider joining the Alpine Club (see page 85 for address).

Chalet-style hotels cluster around the village church in the Tyrolean mountaineering center of Obergurgl.

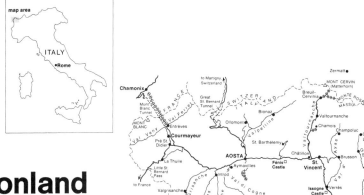

Italy's Alpine vacationland

Visit this historic valley below Europe's highest peaks

High in Italy's northwestern corner, the snowy Alpine peaks and famous resorts of the Valle d'Aosta signal good skiing to winter sports fans. Summer visitors walk in the woods and alpine pastures, go mountain climbing, watch summer skiing at Courmayeur and Breuil-Cervinia, and explore the historic valley towns and Roman ruins.

This is Italy with a French accent, a bilingual region spiced with the rustic zest of the mountains. Qualities of neighboring France and Switzerland blend with the Italian heritage to create a regional mountain identity in food, customs, and architecture. Invaders, too, have left their marks: Celtic tribes, barbarian hordes, Roman legions, Hannibal and his elephants, Napoleon's armies. The French feudal House of Savoy ruled the region for centuries.

You can travel by train to Aosta, where buses fan out into the side valleys. The Valle d'Aosta is connected with Switzerland by the Great St. Bernard Pass and Tunnel and with France by the Little St. Bernard Pass and the Mont Blanc Tunnel.

Make your headquarters in Aosta or in one of the resort towns. In the high valleys you'll find the villagers still clinging to the French language and their pastoral customs.

Roman ruins and high mountains

The motorway crosses the valley from Pont St. Martin along the Dora Báltea River. Feudal castles command the entrances to the tributary valley. You can visit three of the castles – Issogne, Fénis, and Verrès – daily except Monday.

Scattered remnants of the Roman occupation still remain: bridges at Pont St. Martin and Châtillon, an archway and portions of the Roman road at Donnaz, large waterworks at Aymavilles. The largest concentration of ruins is in Aosta, "the Rome of the Alps," where city walls and streets are laid out on the rectangular plan of a military camp. Here you'll see the great arch and gateway, sections of the Roman wall, a bridge, and the remains of the theater.

The highest peaks of the Alps – Mont Blanc, Monte Rosa, Mont Cervin (Matterhorn), and the Gran Para-

Alpine wildflowers carpet the meadows of Valtournanche. Snow-covered Mont Cervin looms in the distance.

diso – fan out along the north, west, and south boundaries of the valley. Major resorts are at Courmayeur, against the bulwark of Mont Blanc (highest mountain in Europe at 15,781 feet); Breuil-Cervinia and Valtournanche, below Mont Cervin; and the Gressoney settlements, which provide access to the Monte Rosa peaks.

A memorable trip by aerial trams links Courmayeur with the French alpine resort of Chamonix. You'll change cabins several times as you glide high over the glaciers of the Mont Blanc massif, reaching a height of nearly 12,500 feet. Other cable cars climb the mountains from Aosta and Breuil-Cervinia.

Southwest of Aosta are the wild ravines of Val Grisanche, Rhêmes, and Val Savaranche, as well as the rich Val di Cogne. Rare European ibex are among the wild animals in the Gran Paradiso National Park. Alpine plants have been collected in the botanic garden at Valnontey.

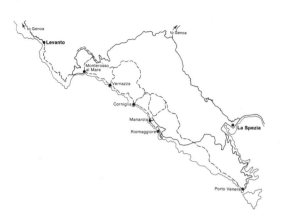

Along the Cinque Terre

Follow the cliffside path from village to village

Five fishing villages—the Cinque Terre or Five Lands of the Italian Riviera—cling to a steep 15-mile section of the Mediterranean coast between Point Mesco and La Spezia. The old customs of the Ligurian fishermen still survive in these isolated cliffside villages, accessible until very recently only by rail and water and linked only by paths.

You catch glimpses of the villages—Monterosso al Mare, Vernazza, Corniglia, Manarola, and Riomaggiore—on a train ride between Genoa and La Spezia. But for a memorable addition to your Italian holiday, leave the train at one of them and walk the footpaths that lead from one village to another.

A seaside pathway cuts across cliffs above the Mediterranean, and an upper pathway threads among terraced vineyards and wooded areas. During the grape harvest,

the upper path is crowded with vineyard workers carrying great baskets of grapes to the villages below. At other seasons of the year, the seaside path linking the villages is more popular.

Villages of the Cinque Terre

Each of the five villages is situated a little differently, its houses and churches (some dating from the 14th century) wedged into the precipitous sea cliffs.

Monterosso al Mare, the largest of the towns, has a fine long beach for swimming and good resort hotels.

Vernazza is perched high on a rocky projection, with a breathtaking view of the Mediterranean. A fort crowns the promontory, and narrow streets lined with colorful old houses radiate from a small square.

Corniglia has tall houses carved from the rock along very narrow streets. The Romanesque church has an elegant rose window.

Manarola, most rugged of the five, perches precariously just out of reach of the crashing waves, its colorful houses clinging to the slope that descends to the dock.

Riomaggiore is crowded into a narrow valley; old houses climb the slopes on either side.

The ridges behind the rugged coast have been transformed into steeply terraced vineyards whose grapes yield a strong, sweet, white wine. High above each settlement is a sanctuary honoring the village's patron saint. Paths lead upward through the vineyards, connecting the upper path with the seaside pathway.

Along the seaside path

One good way to sample this steep, picturesque stretch of coast is to leave the train at Riomaggiore, at the southern end of the string, and follow the path above the sea to Manarola. This part of the path is known as the *Via dell Amore*, or Lover's Walk. You can cover the distance between the two villages—less than a mile—in about 20 minutes. The level flagstone path is bounded on the seaward side by a reassuring guard rail. At Manarola you

Fishing village of Manarola perches on a rocky promontory. Walkway in the foreground is a boat-launching ramp.

Seaside path (left) *cut into the cliff linking the five villages of the Cinque Terre. Boulders occasionally fall onto the pathway; this one damaged the guard rail, but pedestrian traffic was not disrupted. Monterosso* (right) *is the largest of the villages, with a good swimming beach and several resort hotels.*

can decide whether or not you want to continue your walk or wait for the next train.

If you do walk further, you'll find the trail from Manarola to Corniglia unpaved, slightly more rugged, and often littered with fallen rocks; it takes about an hour. The steepest part of the trail is between Corniglia and Vernazza; allow about 1½ hours for this section.

You can walk the 4-mile path between Vernazza and Monterosso in about 1½ hours. During the final part, you descend a steep path to Monterosso with fine views over the town and sea.

The vineyards of the Cinque Terre have been trained low for protection from the wind and to retain the earth's heat for ripening the grapes. Olive, myrtle, cork, and citrus trees are found along this route, along with great bushes of prickly pear with their red fruit and the Mexican agaves with large flowered stalks.

Days of isolation are limited

The absence of a highway has helped to preserve the unhurried and noncommercial atmosphere of the villages, but a new corniche highway being built between La Spezia and Levanto will make the five villages accessible by road.

The new road will pass above the villages, about 450 to 600 feet above the sea, and access roads will descend to the settlements. The corniche road has been completed from La Spezia to Manarola; and the route for the remainder of the road, between Manarola and Monterosso, has been approved.

All five of the villages can be reached by train. All of the local Genoa-La Spezia trains stop in each village, and some direct trains stop at Monterosso.

In summer, excursion boats cruise to the Cinque Terre from Lèrici, Porto Venere, Levanto, and Portofino.

THE WATERWAYS OF EUROPE

Europe's oldest highways were the rivers, on which Bronze Age adventurers first journeyed in search of precious metals. Roman road-builders often built along waterside routes. Centuries later fierce Viking sailors penetrated deeply into western Europe.

For hundreds of years Europe's main rivers—the Danube, Rhine, Seine, Rhône, and Thames—were major routes not only for exploration, but also for transportation and trade. During the Industrial Revolution, systems of canals were built in Britain and on the Continent, linking rivers and lakes, providing a watery network for international commerce.

Today passenger boats have replaced many of the barges which once plied the inland waterways. Well-publicized boat trips cruise the major rivers, as well as many scenic, lesser-known ones. Lake steamers tour the major lakes. Narrow boats cruise the canal networks in England, France, and Holland.

Most of Europe's larger cities are sited on navigable water—on ocean or sea, river, lake, or canal. A harbor tour, canal excursion, lake or river cruise, ferry trip, or island excursion provides welcome relief for the footsore sightseer, as well as new experiences.

In many cities and towns, small boats may be rented by the hour or day for short excursions on rivers and lakes. For example, you can row on the lake in the Bois du Boulogne in Paris, go canoeing on Switzerland's Lake Neuchâtel, row or motor along the Thames from Henley or other towns upriver from London.

Serious sailors may decide to rent a boat for a week or longer, cruising quiet canals, exploring riverside towns, or sailing in coastal waters.

Numerous suggestions for boat trips are listed in the index on page 158. Government tourist offices can provide information on specific excursions.

Ischia...an alternative to Capri

Find solitude or sociability on this green retreat

A pleasant retreat from Europe's crowded cities is Ischia, largest island in the Bay of Naples. Known as the "green island" because of its pine woods and tropical vegetation, Ischia rises above a transparent sea. A two-hour boat ride takes you from Naples to the island's solitary beaches, sociable hotels, domed churches, and ruined castle. Its hilly slopes are laced with vineyards and small villages, while along its roads grow lemon, orange, and olive trees, rose laurel and bougainvillea.

The Greeks settled Ischia in the 5th century B.C. In turn came Syracusans, Romans, Visigoths, Vandals, Ostrogoths, Normans, Angevins, Spaniards, Austrians, and French. Then, finally, came the Italians. The marks of some early settlers still persist, as in the small white houses reminiscent of Arab structures, with outside staircases, domed roofs and crenelated watchtowers.

Ischia's main settlement, Ischia Porto, is beginning to rival neighboring Capri as a popular travel destination, but you can still find solitude elsewhere on the island. Ischia Porto has the most hotels, but the island's most luxurious hostelry is at Lacco Ameno. Simple accommodations are also available in Forio and in the small fishing village of Sant'Angelo for visitors who prefer a quieter vacation.

During the peak travel months from July through September, Italians from the cities in the north seek the sunny southern shores; it is wise to make hotel reservations ahead of time during these months. You can obtain a list of hotels from the Italian Government Travel Office.

If you plan an extended stay, it is often possible to rent a house for a period of time. Some charming villas are hidden beyond rocky paths up the hillsides. Rents depend on the size of the house, the time of year, and location. For information about rentals, write to the Tourist Office, Ischia Porto, Italy.

How to get to Ischia

Boats from Naples make five round trips a day to Ischia, two in the morning and three in the afternoon. The crossing takes about two hours.

If you are driving, you can take your car on the ferry from Pozzuoli, a small town about nine miles west of Naples.

Hydrofoil and helicopter service also run to the island from Naples.

Life on Ischia

Ischia's mild climate is one of its main attractions. In spring the hills are bright with flowers, and by mid-April it's warm enough to swim. If the skies stay clear, the Ischians will tell you, you can swim at midday until December.

Seaside village of Sant'Angelo, its Moorish-style buildings climbing the slope, is on the island's southern coast.

__High above the sea__, villagers live amid citrus groves and terraced vineyards (left). Island with ancient castle, rear, is connected to the mainland by a causeway. From a viewpoint in the pines, you watch the boating activity in Ischia Porto's sheltered harbor (right).

You can choose between busy resort activity or a quiet holiday away from the crowds.

Flat-roofed houses climb Ischia Porto's steep hillside, and narrow streets often turn into a flight of steps. The city's main avenue is lively, with elegant outdoor restaurants, night clubs, and tiny cafes that are crowded and colorful. Smart shops sell play clothes, and you can have a fine pair of sandals made to order in 24 hours. Raffia-work is a local craft.

Ischia Porto has a long white beach, scented pine woods nearby, and thermal baths. The harbor, almost circular in shape, lies in the crater of an extinct volcano. A cable railway climbs to the summit of Mount Epomeo, the island's highest point at 2,585 feet.

Neighboring Ischia Ponte is named for the causeway linking the coast with a rocky island, topped by the half-ruined 15th-century Aragonese castle and several churches. From July to September, the castle is open to visitors; excavated objects and other items associated with the castle's history are housed in a small museum. From the esplanade in front of the castle, you have a splendid view of the Bay of Naples.

Beyond Ischia Porto you'll find numerous good beaches. One of the best is at San Francesco, a tiny village about 20 minutes by bus from Ischia Porto; another is at Citara, about 40 minutes away.

Seeing the island

Many visitors never get beyond Ischia Porto, but distances are so short that it is easy to explore some of the island's other attractions. You can tour the coast road to visit some of the smaller villages, lie on a sandy beach, splash in the sea, or perhaps take off on a skin-diving excursion.

The road around the island winds among the vineyards and passes beaches with caves hewn in the rock. Occasionally a small white village, Moorish in appearance, comes into view. The white cottages are sometimes roofed with a dome and often have outside staircases; vines climb the outer walls.

You can drive around the island (about 20 miles) in less than two hours in your own car, or you can hire a car with driver. There is good bus service. For local sightseeing, Vespa taxis carry passengers in parasol-shaded sidecars, or you can take a more leisurely ride in an open cab drawn by horses wearing splendid straw hats, adorned with plumes and flowers.

The scenic road circling the island follows the northern coast from Ischia Porto to the fashionable spa-resorts of Casamicciola and neighboring Lacco Ameno. Offshore is Il Fungo, an unusual mushroom-shaped rock. The village of Forio is perched on a promontory on the island's western coast; at the end of the road is the small Punta del Succorso Church.

Another good view is from La Guardiola, accessible by a short footpath from Panza. Just east of Panza, a side road descends to the fishing village of Sant'Angelo. The winding road along the southern slope of Mount Epomeo provides many fine views over the island and coast. If you've brought along a picnic, you can have a pleasant lunch beneath the pines.

Touring the heel of Italy's boot

A touch of the Arabian nights in the Apulian hills

Only the most intrepid travelers venture deep into southern Italy to the region of Apulia, stretching along the Adriatic shore. In the heel of Italy's boot, you'll discover fantasy villages where each whitewashed house is topped by a conical dome and hex signs are painted on the stone roof tiles.

From the rounded hills above the Itria valley, between the port cities of Bari and Brindisi, groups of the cone-topped *trulli* dot the ochre and green landscape. The district extends from Monopoli and Castellana Grotte on the north to Martina Franca on the south.

The most spectacular display of the *trulli* is found in Alberobello, where more than a thousand of the unusual buildings climb the side of a wooded hill along narrow flagstone streets. With tiled domes pointing skyward, the whole town suggests a fanciful garden city created by a master magician.

Traveling in Apulia

You can rent a car in either Bari or Brindisi to drive to the *trulli* district. If you travel to Apulia by train, Bari is the terminus of the long Rome-Bari rail line, local service extending north and south along the coast.

Both of the cities can also be reached by air. For travelers arriving or departing by ship, Brindisi is the terminus for ferry service to Corfu and Greece.

You'll find Apulia a more prosperous region than its neighbors; land is cultivated wherever irrigation permits, and the vineyards and olive groves on the Apulian plateaus and plains contrast with the sun-baked scenery elsewhere in southern Italy.

Avoid the region in summer and winter, for weather extremes make traveling uncomfortable. It is most pleasant in the spring, when everything is in bloom, or during the mild fall months.

The *trulli* and their origin

A strange, white, dry-stone structure with a domed tile roof, the *trullo* is the typical peasant house of the region. In the countryside they stand in groups of three or four, easily identified by the conical roofs pointing skyward.

The origin of the dwellings is somewhat obscure. The primitive buildings show traces of the prehistoric Saracen and early Christian civilizations. They also have elements of ritual and magic beliefs. Some experts think the unusual shape was adapted from the tents the invading Saracens used in their desert homeland.

Each house is built on a square plan. The loose-laid walls have no mortar and are plastered a dazzling white with lime wash. Crowning each building is the pointed dome, covered with concentric, weathered slabs of the smooth local gray stone (also loose laid) known as *chiancarelle*, and closed by a slender finial. Some of the upper walls are decorated with statues or crosses, and you'll often see astrological and religious symbols traced in lime on the stone tiles of the domes.

The doorway is a rounded arch surmounted by a rustic gable; often a bird cage hangs near the entrance.

Conical roofs of scattered whitewashed trulli dot the countryside near the Apulian village of Selva di Fasano.

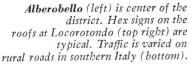

Alberobello (left) is center of the district. Hex signs on the roofs at Locorotondo (top right) are typical. Traffic is varied on rural roads in southern Italy (bottom).

Inside, each building consists of a large central room; the hearth and various small alcoves, serving as rooms, are set into the thick walls. A central chimney serves each building, an outside staircase giving the family access to the attic.

A visit to Alberobello

Center of the trulli district is the hilly town of Alberobello, about 35 miles south of Bari, where virtually the entire town is composed of the unusual white buildings.

The most characteristic quarter of Alberobello is the "Zona Monumentale," lying on a wooded slope to the south, beyond a mall. The quarter is white with trulli, each with its dry stone roof.

As you walk through the town, look for hex signs painted on the domes. The dark-garbed ladies of the town often sit in front of their houses, weaving mats and shawls from threads hung on nails. In the upper part of the quarter, you'll see the Church of Sant'Antonio, also in the form of a trullo.

Away from the Adriatic, accommodations are limited, but visitors who wish to stop overnight will find the Albergo dei Trulli in Alberobello. Like the rest of the town, the hotel follows the traditional conical architecture. On warm days, luncheon is served on the terrace in the garden under a large, bright awning.

As you drive through the region, you'll have good views from the hills of the trulli-dotted landscape, particularly near Selva di Fasano and from the Locorotondo-Martina Franca road. Vineyards and olive orchards grow in the umber-colored soil, and each plot of farmland has its white farmhouse, topped by the distinctive cone roofs and marked with hex signs to ward off evil spirits.

The caves of Castellana

North of Alberobello, about 25 miles from Bari, are the largest and most noted caves in Italy, those of the Castellana. You can visit the caves daily; both short and long tours are conducted periodically. In the numerous chambers you'll see "draperies," along with richly-colored stalactites and stalagmites.

A good way to sample Sicily

You can swim, ski, explore ruins, or visit a volcano

Why has Sicily attracted European tourists for centuries? They have been lured by its dramatic scenery, colorful folk life, moderate prices, and Greek ruins that are generally better preserved than any ruins in Greece itself.

Sicily is popular in all seasons except summer, when *sirocco* winds from Africa sometimes make the island uncomfortably hot. You'll see it at its best from January to June.

If you don't have time to visit the entire island, you'll find the eastern coast—across from the toe of Italy—a very satisfactory sample. Airlines serve Catánia from several Italian cities. Trains and automobiles are ferried across the Strait of Messina from Reggio Calabria, and hydrofoils also make the crossing to Messina. Bus service links the coastal towns.

The strategically-sited Mediterranean island was the crossroads and melting pot—and often the battleground—of the ancient world. Ruins dating back more than 25 centuries chronicle its ties to ancient Greece and the subsequent civilizations which visited its shores.

Few cities can match Taormina's natural site on a lofty terrace above the sea, Mount Etna looming in the background. The beaches lie below the town, down several miles by winding road, but you'll find bus service frequent. The town's main street, the Corso, retains the feeling of a village in its colorful activity and lively sociability. Plays are still performed in the Greek theater, but you may want to visit its site just for the view.

Busy Catánia is the major commercial center, a city of dignified buildings and wide squares and streets. Resort areas lie north and south along the coast.

Mount Etna's immense cone, snow-capped much of the year, dominates all of eastern Sicily. In less than an hour you can drive from Catánia to Etna's slopes, then continue by cableway to the base of the main crater. Or you can travel around the peak by road or rail; drive or take the Circum-Etna railway from Catánia, climbing through charming hill towns and long-cooled lava fields to Randazzo, then returning to the coast near Giarre.

Siracusa once rivaled Athens as a wealthy bastion of Greek civilization. Its Greek ruins are dominated by the graceful theater, where classical dramas are performed.

The Aeolian Islands

From Messina or Milazzo you can travel by boat to the Aeolian Islands, a sun-blessed archipelago in the clear blue sea north of Sicily. Boats also connect the islands with Palermo and Naples. Not yet overrun with tourists, the islands offer a quiet interlude where you can go underwater exploring and fishing in a fantastic submarine world, visit the volcano of Stromboli, wander through ancient ruins, or explore the islands by boat or on foot.

Largest of the seven islands is Lipari. Its charming little town makes a good base for trips to the other islands. Simple accommodations are also available on the islands of Stromboli, Panarea, and Vulcano.

Greek theater *overlooks the resort town of Taormina, with cloud-topped Mount Etna in the background.*

Sandy beaches rim sheltered bays at Paleokastritsa (top and right); olive and cypress trees cover the island's rugged hills. From Kanoni viewpoint, you gaze on an island monastery and Mouse Island (left). Small boats anchor in canal-moat near Venetian fort (center).

Seeing the town

Part of Corfu's charm evolves from the combined influence of the island's former rulers. The narrow streets of the old city are reminiscent of Venice, green-shuttered, tall white houses with lines of drying wash strung above the street. The arcades facing the Plateia, modeled after those along the Rue de Rivoli in Paris, were built by Napoleon's troops. British rule left the elegant Royal Palace, the game of cricket (played with some local rule modifications), and a taste for English ginger beer (locally called *tsintsibira*).

Strike out on foot to explore the town. Wander through the busy old quarter, with its tiny shops and sidewalk vendors. Saunter through the open-air market, where buyers and sellers haggle over the fruits and vegetables. Visit the cool, incense-laden church of St. Spiridion, reposing place of Corfu's patron saint. Walk to one of the fortresses for a view over the city. Examine archaeological finds and Oriental art in the local museum. Stroll along the arcaded Esplanade.

You can walk beyond town to the wooded park and the villa of Mon Repos, once a home of the Greek royal family (Prince Philip, the Duke of Edinburgh, was born here). Further along the coast, about 2 miles from town, is the Kanoni viewpoint. Its famous panorama, immortalized by many painters, takes in the shimmering lagoon with a white monastery set on a tiny island and the nearby wooded island of Pontikonisi (Mouse Island) rising abruptly from the water.

Around the island

Tranquillity is perhaps Corfu's greatest appeal. In town you can arrange for a rental car, bicycle, or motorbike; or inquire about local bus service to various villages.

Once you venture into the lush countryside, island aromas surround you — a potpourri of orange and lemon, myrtle and thyme. Roses, clematis, and marguerites grow wild, and unpruned olive trees reach heights of almost fifty feet. You drive through rugged mountains that threaten to crowd the road into the sea. To the north, silvery olive trees grow to the water's edge at Dassia, site of a Club Méditerranée resort.

West of Corfu you drive between orange and olive groves to the island's most famous beauty spot, Paleokastritsa, with its sheltered twin bays and sandy beaches. Legends claim Odysseus, King of Ithaca, was shipwrecked on this wild coast. Plan to watch the sunset from the promontory at Pélakas, where you can see both coasts.

The road south brings you to the village of Gastouri, nestling among trees, and to the Achilleion Palace, now a casino. Built by the Empress Elizabeth of Austria, and later the summer retreat of Kaiser Wilhelm II, the palace is a hodge-podge of architectural styles and statues, its lush garden stretching down to the sea.

Along the coastal road, the attractive fishing village of Benitses makes a pleasant stop. Korissia Lagoon, with its sand dunes and beach, is ideal for a picnic. Since it's off the main road, you'll have to go part way on foot.

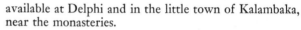

The monasteries of Meteora

You climb rocky stairways to ancient refuges

Many surprises unfold for the traveler in Greece, but surely the strange medieval monasteries of Meteora must rank high on the list. Founded by hermits during the 14th century as Serbs and Byzantines battled for control of the rich Thessalian plain, the rock buildings cap a strange forest of gigantic rock pillars rising abruptly above the northwestern end of the valley. Here the hermits could meditate, undisturbed by the warfare below.

On a three-day trip from Athens, you can visit the ruins of Delphi, then continue north through the Greek countryside to Meteora. Overnight accommodations are available at Delphi and in the little town of Kalambaka, near the monasteries.

If you drive, you'll find the road good, but narrow and winding. Many road signs are in English as well as Greek, but be sure to get detailed directions before you start out. Guided bus tours from Athens go to Meteora, or you can also hire a car with a driver-guide.

Spring is the best season for traveling in this part of Greece, before summer's heat arrives. In April and May the towering, jagged mountains encircling the Thessalian plain are still covered with snow, almond and peach trees are in bloom, fields are green with new growth, and red poppies add bright accents to the landscape.

Through the Greek countryside

You'll catch many delightful glimpses of Greek country life along the route. You may round a corner to see a family preparing its noonday meal (maybe even barbecuing a whole goat on a spit set up along the roadside). Women are outside washing clothes in large, square, wooden tubs. Donkeys plod along the road, laden with everything from little boys to bundles of firewood and jugs of wine. If you're fortunate, you may see a Greek wedding party, happily singing and dancing its progressive way from the groom's house to the *taverna* to the bride's house and on to the church.

The road north passes through the prosperous provincial town of Lamia, then makes its way northwest across the vast plain. From Karditsa a fine straight road continues to Trikala; Kalambaka is another 20 miles beyond.

Then the road begins to climb steeply until you are several hundred feet above the valley: the view back over the plain is lovely. Suddenly you are confronted with rock walls of giant perpendicular pillars—the Meteora.

The Meteora

Because the fertile plain of Thessaly was once covered by a large inland sea, the water's erosive power split and

Bridge spans the chasm, and rocky steps lead up to the monastery. It's a bit of a climb but not dangerous.

Meteora's monasteries perch atop these perpendicular cliffs; five of the ancient retreats can be visited. When you finally reach the top of the rocky stair, you have a magnificent view over the plain of Thessaly.

shaped the rocks into their strange forms. They appear like three or four-hundred-foot boulders tossed atop the hills—the Greeks thought they had been thrown there by angry gods.

While medieval warriors struggled for control of the rich valley, a monastery was founded on the Great Meteoron. Other hermitages evolved into monasteries, until finally 24 rose atop the black rocks. Women were excluded, and austere rules were imposed on the inhabitants. Today only five of the monasteries remain.

At one time, the only way to reach the monasteries was to be pulled up in a rope basket which the monks, turning a windlass, raised from the top, or by climbing a jointed ladder let down from above. Today, a road winds near the base of the cliffs, and you climb steps cut in the rock to reach the monasteries. The stone stairways, although sometimes long and steep, are not dangerous to climb.

Visiting the monasteries

Some of the monasteries are historical monuments; others still function as working monasteries. Five can be visited —if you have the time and endurance. Although some are quite near each other, you must descend from one pinnacle and then climb another to reach the next monastery.

The most spectacular of the group is the Great Meteoron, atop an almost perpendicular cliff and reached by a strenuous climb. Its massive gate opens on a large courtyard. The cloister, churches, and refectory symbolize a way of life, now almost extinct, when religious fervor inspired infinite labor, discomfort, and self-denial.

A drawbridge connects Aghios Stephanos to the main cliff. Some of the old treasures—wood carvings and a few icons—have been preserved, but most of the religious relics no longer exist. From the windows you have a marvelous view over the plain: the Aegean is barely discernable on the horizon; to the west rise the snowy Pindus Mountains, to the northeast Mount Olympus, mythical home of the Greek gods.

Aghia Trias is situated atop a particularly forbidding pinnacle, reached by a steep climb up a flight of steps cut into the rocky face.

One of the retreats, Aghia Roussani, is now a convent. Located on the lowest rock, it is less difficult to reach than most of the monasteries.

Largest of the retreats is fortress-like Aghios Varlaam, one of the later monasteries founded in the 16th century. Here you'll find restored frescoes in the Chapel of All Saints and a library still retaining some manuscripts.

The Monastery of Metamorfosis, founded in the 14th century, has a guest house and restaurant for tourists; it is open from April through October.

Try the simple life on Kos

The pace is relaxed on this Greek holiday island

The Dodecanese islands, scattered off the southwestern coast of Turkey, have remained relatively untouched by modern civilization. If you're seeking a spot to spend an inexpensive, carefree holiday, the island of Kos is an ideal choice. Located northwest of larger and more cosmopolitan Rhodes, Kos is accessible by air from Athens or by steamer from Piræus. Boats connect it with neighboring islands and with the Turkish city of Bodrum.

Plan your visit between April and October; mellow autumn is perhaps the most delightful season, when days are long, the sun warm, and most of the vacationers have vanished.

Most of the island's hotels and restaurants are located in the island's main city, also called Kos. Cypress and palm trees line the city's paved roads, and flowering oleander and hibiscus provide festive color. A fort built by the Crusaders still stands at the harbor entrance. The city's modern European-style buildings—built following a destructive 1933 earthquake—present an unusual contrast to the traditional, close-quartered buildings of most Aegean island cities.

Even in midsummer a relaxed pace prevails. You spend days swimming in the warm Aegean, sunning on the tree-lined sandy beach, or leisurely touring the island. Bicycles and motor scooters can be rented at modest cost.

Some of the most enjoyable *tavernas* are those lining the waterfront. You sit outside at a vine-shaded table, chatting with friends over plates of *moussaka* and watching fishermen unload their daily catch. In the evening, sip *ouzo* or island wine in one of the tavernas while listening to Greek music. (The tavernas seldom get going until June, however, the musicians retreating to Rhodes or Athens during the cold winter months.)

The museum contains a statue of Hippocrates, father of medicine, who was born on the island in 460 B.C. Local folk claim he meditated and treated the sick in the shade of an ancient-but-still-standing plane tree.

About 2½ miles from town on a terraced hillside are the ruins of the Asclepeion, the sanctuary of Asclepios, god of medicine. Pilgrims traveled here over 2,000 years ago to seek the healing waters of warm springs.

Exploring the island

Take local buses or hire a taxi when you set off to explore the island. Mountains form a high ridge along most of its 45-mile length. Most of the settlements perch along the northern slopes, villagers descending to cultivate the plain below. Asfendiou, high in the mountains west of Kos, looks north along the sprawling coast of Asia Minor. Rampant tomato vines and olive groves supply a local tomato paste factory.

The busy fishing village of Kardamaina, almost isolated by mountains, lies on the southern coast. Artesian wells furnish water for gardens. In summer, caiques laden with fruit, garden vegetables, and fish depart from the jetty for small nearby islands.

At the western end of the island is the fishing village of Kefalos, where village dwellings crown a rocky knoll overlooking a natural cove.

Fishermen *prepare their rigs for the next trip. Boats sail in late afternoon, returning in early morning.*

IN GREECE: special interests

BOAT TRIPS TO GREEK ISLANDS • If you enjoy the sea, you'll find almost limitless possibilities for boat trips among the hundreds of islands which lie off the coast of Greece.

Regularly scheduled cruises leave from the port of Piræus for different island groups. You can make day cruises to Aegina and Hydra, trips lasting two or three days that visit Delos and Mykonos or Rhodes, or longer trips that stop at a number of islands. Extended cruises, lasting one to two weeks or more, visit ports of neighboring countries as well. Many of the cruises include conducted sightseeing trips ashore.

Should you prefer to concentrate on one or two islands, steamship lines operate an inter-island network from Piræus connecting major islands in the Saronic Gulf and the Aegean. If you wish to take your car, ferry service is available to many islands.

CHARTERING A YACHT • Perhaps you prefer to plan your own itinerary for a cruise among the Greek islands on your own yacht complete with crew. You can arrange to charter a yacht through your travel agent or a yacht chartering agency. Work out the details with them several months in advance. You'll find a wide range of yacht sizes and an equally wide range of prices; the cost is determined by your budget, the number of passengers, length of time, and itinerary. You can obtain information on chartering from Charterers Association and Yacht Experts, P.O. B 341, Piraeus, Greece.

XENIA HOTELS AND MOTELS • Moderately-priced accommodations in the Greek provinces and on many of the islands are provided by Xenia (meaning "hospitality") hotels and motels, built and regularly checked by the national tourist organization. These modern accommodations are found in many places of interest.

MUSEUM SEASON TICKET • A three-month season ticket admitting the visitor to Greece's museums and archaeological sites can be purchased from the Archaeological Funds and Expropriations Office, 17 Filellinon Street, Athens.

GREEK TAVERNAS • Where is the best place to discover authentic Greek cooking in an atmosphere of hospitality and merriment? The *taverna*, an institution as old as Greece itself.

Often you'll first hear the melancholy music of the *bouzouki*, guiding you into the simple building with its hand-hewn wooden tables lining rough, whitewashed walls. Usually there is no menu; you walk into the kitchen, peer into baskets of fresh fish and vegetables and the pots simmering on the stove, then order your meal by pointing at the container whose contents most appeal to you.

Each *taverna* has its regular customers who sip piquant, anise-flavored *ouzo* or the pungent, resinated Greek wine *retsina* while enjoying music and companionship. Often the music ignites spontaneous singing and vigorous dancing.

CAVE-EXPLORING • More than 5,200 caves have been discovered in Greece, and eight of the best are now open to the public: the Koutouki cave, near Paeania, south of Athens; the Perama caves, near Ioannina in northwestern Greece; the three caves at the Mani, along the bay of Dyros, south of Sparta; the Draggorati cave on the Ionian island of Cephalonia; the cave of Petrolona, near Thessaloniki; and the cave on the island of Antiparos in the Cyclades.

HANDICRAFT EXHIBITION • A permanent showroom of Greek handicrafts is located in Athens at 9 Mitropoleos Street, near Snytagma Square. Organized by the National Association of Greek Handicrafts, the exhibit displays examples of all types of Greek popular art, including hand-woven textiles, embroidery, carpets and rugs, pottery, metalwork, and woodworking.

GREEK CUISINE • The foods of Greece share many similarities with the cuisines of other Eastern Mediterranean countries that were once part of the Ottoman Empire. Hotels and larger restaurants usually feature international cooking, supplemented with a few Greek specialties. You'll find authentic Greek dishes more readily available in the simple tavernas. The Greek National Tourist Office can provide suggestions on some of the Greek food specialties.

OPEN-AIR PERFORMANCES • During the summer, Greek dramas, opera, music, and ballet are performed at open-air theaters in Athens; at Epidavros, south of Corinth; at Dodoni, south of Ioannina in northwestern Greece; at Philippi, near the Macedonian city of Kavala; on the island of Thassos; and at Diou in the Mount Olympus area.

From April through October, Sound and Light performances are presented in Athens at the Acropolis, in Rhodes at the Palace of the Grand Masters, and in Corfu.

GREEK EASTER FESTIVITIES • Easter is the year's most important holiday in Greece, beginning with three weeks of pre-Lenten Carnival, followed by seven weeks of Lent, and culminating in Easter festivities that continue for a full week. If you plan to be in Greece at this time, check the date; the Eastern Orthodox Church celebrates Easter on a different date from other faiths.

In Athens much of the pre-Lenten and Easter gaiety can be observed in the Plaka, the old city hugging the slopes just below the Acropolis. Here there will be feasting, dancing, and singing, along with the traditional masquerade parties. Throughout Greece, Good Friday is a time for candlelight processions; other special religious services are held Saturday night and Easter Sunday. The following week brings more feasting and dancing, featuring special dance performances in many areas.

Greek National Tourist Organization offices
645 Fifth Avenue, New York, N.Y. 10022
627 West 6th Street, Los Angeles, Calif. 90017

Along Spain's Cantabrian coast

Detour to prehistoric art caves and a medieval village

Donkeys and oxen still plod the rural roads along the northern coast of Spain, in the lovely and often-bypassed region known as the Cantabrian Coast. A coastal road edges the blue Bay of Biscay, connecting the resorts and fishing villages where Europeans spend their summer holidays. Yet not far away are prehistoric caves, a medieval town, and unspoiled Basque villages.

Here you have the blue sea on the north, the snow-streaked Cantabrian mountain range to the south, and green valleys between—the perfect place to unwind and adapt to the slow-paced Spanish tempo. Before long, afternoon siestas and late dining hours are taken for granted.

Since the golden sand beaches along this coast are a summer refuge from the inland heat, you'll find resort cities crowded. Advance reservations are necessary if you visit during July and August.

The Basque country

Once you cross the Bidasoa River from France into Spain, ox-drawn carts become a standard part of the view. This is one of the oldest inhabited areas of Europe: ancestors of the Basques lived in these mountains when Iberian tribes invaded the Peninsula. Secondary roads lead up the coastal valleys to Basque villages, where clean white buildings, topped by red roofs, cluster against the verdant hills.

To catch the flavor of the region quickly, take the side road from Irún to Fuenterrabía. This well-preserved village at the mouth of the Bidasoa has a lively and colorful fishermen's quarter, as well as the characteristic wooden houses and imposing mansions. The Castle of Charles V is now a comfortable *parador*, or government-run hotel.

Handsome San Sebastián, with its famed semi-circular beach, is Spain's summer capital. Activity is at its height in August, when the best matadors perform at San Sebastián's bull fights and the best *pelota* (Basque ball) players compete at the Fronton. But the weather will be hot (up to 90°) and the town will be crowded. After 6 in the evening, people begin to stroll on the beaches, and nurses are still pushing prams at 9 o'clock. Afterwards, dinner is both late and long.

Attractive fishing villages, excellent beaches, and quiet summer resorts are scattered along the coast between San Sebastián and Bilbao.

Guetaria is a rugged, traditional fishing village, built on a rocky promontory that thrusts into the sea. Steep streets tunnel under houses. In a chapel built into the rock on one of these subterranean streets, a candle burns for Guetaria's men at sea. Watch for the turnoff beyond Lequeitio to Elanchove, a village that literally hangs down the side of the cliff.

Bilbao is the other great city along the Basque coast, a trading and seafaring city since its earliest days. You'll

Farm family harvests the summer hay crop. Fringed headdress on oxen keeps flies and gnats from their eyes.

Many fine swimming beaches line the Cantabrian coastline, including this broad stretch at Suances (left), west of Santander. Weathered church of Santa Illana faces a quiet plaza in the medieval village of Santillana del Mar (right). Statue of saint is nestled in niche above the door.

find more good beaches and inviting coastal towns on the way to Santander.

Prehistoric cave paintings

Preserved on the walls and ceilings of more than a dozen caverns in Santander province are paintings, drawings, and engravings created 12,000 to 20,000 years ago. The two most interesting caves are accessible to visitors: the famed painted cave of Altamira (west of Santander, near Santillana) and El Castillo (south of Santander, near the village of Puente Viesgo).

Altamira's art exhibit consists of about 150 pictures representing the Old Stone Age. The largest and best are grouped in one low-ceilinged chamber, measuring about 60 by 30 feet. As the guide plays his light across the ceiling, an astonishing herd of beasts emerges from the shadows, each painted with such realism and vigor that it seems to surge with life and movement. The colors—mostly deep red, sepia, ochre, and smoky black—appear as fresh and strong as though applied only a few days ago.

El Castillo is somewhat less spectacular from an artistic standpoint, but it is dramatically superior as a cavern. Galleries lead you through unearthly forests of stalagmites, past petrified cascades and shimmering limestone draperies, to great chambers hung with stalactites. The art of El Castillo is scattered throughout the grotto's murky length; more than 130 pictures of bison, deer, wild horses, and bulls have been identified.

Santillana del Mar

As you walk the cobblestone streets of Santillana del Mar, it is easy to feel you have stepped back in time 500 years. In the quiet plaza near a fine medieval church, you can watch a herdsman water his cows at an ancient stone trough beside the public pool where women kneel to scrub their laundry. An ox-drawn cart rumbles toward you over the stones of the narrow street—so narrow that you must step aside into the protection of a doorway.

Handsome stone mansions, once the town houses of noble families, line the village streets. The town's architectural treasure is the Church of Santa Illana. Though not large, it is classed as one of the best Romanesque structures in Spain.

Today about a thousand people live here, their simple farm life scarcely changed in a dozen generations. To preserve its medieval character, the village is now a national historic monument. Most of the impressive manor houses date from the 15th century. Many are open to visitors; some are occupied by shops. But this is a farming village, and you encounter the signs and aromas of farming activity everywhere.

The government has turned a medieval mansion into a modern hotel, the Parador Gil Blas. The furniture is old Spanish provincial, and in the bedrooms, heavy shuttered doors, set in walls three feet thick, open to wrought-iron balconies. In summer, advance reservations are advisable, and the length of stay is limited to 10 days.

✓ACROSS EUROPE WITH SIGN LANGUAGE

If you're planning a motoring trip for part or all of your European visit, never fear: you can understand the traffic signs even if you can't understand the language. Most European countries use a set of graphic symbols on road signs, avoiding the confusion of Europe's differing languages. As a result, signs through most of Europe are simple, bold, diagrammatic, and very easy to follow.

Most American drivers have little trouble making the changeover to the symbolic signs. But embarrassing complications sometimes plague the foreign visitor who violates prohibitive signs, so it's wise to study them until you can recognize them quickly on the road. Illustrations of the signs are provided on many maps and in some travel guides. If you are renting a car, the company may have a folder of signs available.

The international signs are based on geometric shapes: triangle, circle, and rectangle. The colors are bold—red, white, blue, and black. Most countries use the same symbols, although there may be variations in color combinations and arrangements.

Highway signs ● Red triangular signs call attention to dangers ahead. The danger is illustrated by a black symbol on a white background. These signs may announce curves, steep slopes, slippery or rough roads, rights of way, pedestrian or animal crossings, traffic lights, falling rocks, road repair, or railroad crossings.

Red circles convey definite driving instructions, usually prohibitions. A red circle with a white center means "road closed to vehicles." A circle with a white bar means "no entry in this direction"; it's probably a one-way street. A black symbol on white background

inside the circle shows what is prohibited; signs may give speed limits, prohibit passing, show compulsory right of way. A similar roadsign cut by a diagonal line means the prohibition has ended.

The common stop sign is a red circle enclosing a red triangle with STOP in black on a white background. The use of "stop" is now internationally accepted.

A blue circle with white sign indicates compulsory instructions—the route to follow, the direction to proceed around a traffic circle, minimum speed, pedestrian or cycle routes.

Rectangular signs give information. Usually blue with the symbol in white, or against a white background, they indicate such conveniences as parking, gas stations, telephones, and first aid stations. Distances, road numbers, and directions appear on rectangular signs. Schematic maps provide advance directions for crossroads or turnoffs for complex junctions.

In the city ● Many of the same signs are used in the cities and towns, but you'll also encounter a few new ones. A red circle enclosing a blue center means no stopping if the center is cut by a red X, no parking if the center is slashed by a red diagonal bar.

Some signs require local knowledge, as well as a bit of the language. In cities, often you can park in certain areas only with a parking card (check the glove compartment of your rental car); you set it for the time you arrive and park, and the card indicates when you must return to the car. Other signs specify parking on alternate sides of the street on alternate days (odd or even-numbered days), with the parking times given in the 24-hour clock.

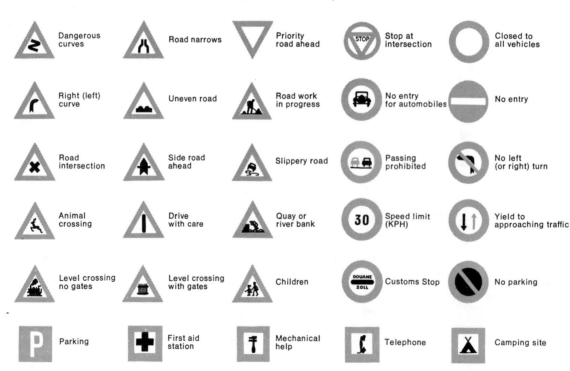

Dangerous curves	Road narrows	Priority road ahead	Stop at intersection	Closed to all vehicles
Right (left) curve	Uneven road	Road work in progress	No entry for automobiles	No entry
Road intersection	Side road ahead	Slippery road	Passing prohibited	No left (or right) turn
Animal crossing	Drive with care	Quay or river bank	Speed limit (KPH)	Yield to approaching traffic
Level crossing no gates	Level crossing with gates	Children	Customs Stop	No parking
Parking	First aid station	Mechanical help	Telephone	Camping site

A visit to medieval Spain

On a day's outing from Madrid—historic Segovia

The atmosphere of medieval Spain pervades the hill town of Segovia, only 1½ hours by car from Madrid. In its crooked, crowded streets—many too narrow for cars—you sense an air of the Spanish Middle Ages.

Relatively small and compact, Segovia is pleasant for walking. Soft, clear light washes over its ochre-colored buildings and red tile roofs. Small houses—decorated with iron grill work and flowers—and Romanesque churches are scattered along the narrow streets and small squares. Facing the Cathedral is the Plaza Franco, Segovia's main square, with side streets radiating from it.

Three historic structures reflect aspects of Segovia's past: the aqueduct, the Alcazar, and the Cathedral.

Built of huge, uncemented blocks of granite, the majestic arches of the Roman aqueduct have towered over Segovia for nearly 2000 years. A graceful double tier of arches rises more than 90 feet above the Plaza Azoguejo, supporting a conduit which still carries water to the town from the distant Fuenfria mountains.

One of medieval Spain's great fortress-castles, the romantic Alcazar crowns a rocky spur above converging river valleys. Isabella was proclaimed Queen of Castile in its throne room, and in 1505 Columbus made his will here, King Ferdinand acting as a witness.

Before you cross the drawbridge over the moat, walk along the curving terrace and gaze over the valley. Looking up, you see the castle's pointed turrets, with the battlemented central tower rising above.

Segovia's elegant 16th-century Cathedral occupies a place of honor above the town. Splendid stained glass windows, carved choir stalls, wrought-iron chapel gates, and fine tapestries distinguish the interior. Don't miss the Gothic cloisters and the museum.

The Castilian countryside

On a trip to Segovia from Madrid, you cross the pinewood covered Guadarrama Mountains by one of two routes, over the Guadarrama Pass (or through the tunnel) or via the Navacerrada Pass and La Granja.

One of Spain's showplaces, the royal hunting lodge of La Granja was built by the homesick Bourbon King Philip V to remind him of Versailles. Formal gardens with fountains surround the castle.

If you can extend your excursion by a day or two, seek out more of Castile's famed castles. For a map and information on castles in the province of Segovia, stop at the town's tourist office (Plaza de Franco 8).

The medieval fortress town of Avila, completely encircled by solid walls, is a monument to St. Teresa, founder of many of Spain's religious institutions, who was born here in 1515. To the southwest, the Sierra de Gredos range is a sportsman's paradise, offering mountain climbing, fishing, and hunting.

A detour to El Escorial brings back the grim days of the Inquisition. Built by Philip II in the late 16th century as palace, monastery, and mausoleum, El Escorial was a bulwark against heresy, proclaiming the absolutism of the monarchy and the Church.

Not far from El Escorial is the Valley of the Fallen, a monument to Spanish Civil War dead. A cathedral built inside the mountain houses Francisco Franco's tomb.

Segovia's Cathedral (left) towers over the town, while the famed Alcazar (right) dominates the countryside.

Festive Andalusia

Moorish towns—a feast of sights and sounds

Nowhere in Spain will you be more immersed in lively celebrations than in fiesta-loving Andalusia, where religious fervor and a love of festivity combine in colorful *ferias* and fiestas. This sunny land gazes south toward Africa, many towns of gleaming white reflecting the centuries of Moorish occupation.

In a week you can merely sample its charms—flower-filled Seville, the sherry *bodegas* of Jerez, whitewashed mountain towns, lovely Málaga and the Costa del Sol resorts, the Moorish grandeur of Granada and Córdoba.

Andalusia is best enjoyed in seasons other than summer, when it is hot. Spring is the festive time, the processions of Holy Week followed by local celebrations. Bull-

fight season runs from late March through October.

In the cities, plan to do your major sightseeing in the morning, so you can adapt to the Spanish schedule: dining late (see page 131), relaxing during the hot afternoons, squandering a delicious hour in a cafe, strolling in the warm magic of an Andalusian night.

Buses link the main towns, but you'll see the country best by car. Main roads are two-lane and paved, sometimes pockmarked. Mountain highways are steep, winding, and slow. Gas stations are not numerous, so don't stretch your luck. In the cities, park your car and do your sightseeing on foot or by horse-drawn cart.

Fairs and fiestas

The tremendous spectacle of Holy Week celebrations attracts many visitors to Seville, Granada, and Málaga. (Make hotel reservations well in advance.) Social life slows to a halt, and penitents parade through the streets, holding aloft Crucifixion tableaux and images of saints.

Spring is the time of the region's big fairs: April in Seville, May in Jerez and Córdoba, June in Granada. Best known is Seville's week-long *feria*, celebrated by parades, bullfights, horse races, music, and *flamenco* dancing.

During the week before Pentecost (Whitsun), festive cavalcades of horsemen and flower-garlanded wagons make the annual pilgrimage along Andalusian backroads, heading for Almonte and the El Rocio *romería*.

Seville to the sea

Fabled Seville is an oasis in Andalusia's parched interior. Elegant gardens, parks, and cascading blooms perfume and brighten the city.

Many of the city's attractions lie within walking distance: the handsome Giralda bell tower, the massive cathedral, the rambling palaces of the Alcazar. Nearby is the former tobacco factory that served as one of the settings in the opera *Carmen*. Friends rendezvous along the Calle de la Sierpes. Most colorful of the local quar-

Whitewashed parador dominates this view of Arcos de la Frontera, perched high above the Guadalete River canyon.

Andalusia's cities delight visitors with luxuriant parks and gardens and many festive celebrations. Delicate water displays highlight the elegant Moorish gardens of Granada's Generalife (left). Horsemen parade during Seville's great April fair (right).

ters is the Santa Cruz district, a delightful labyrinth of twisting alleys, tiny squares, and secluded courtyards.

The road south leads to elegant Jerez, where sherries are blended and aged (see page 131). Sparkling white Cadiz, cradling its huge natural harbor, has been a busy, boisterous seaport since Roman times.

The road to Ronda

The bumpy road east from Jerez penetrates Andalusia's little-known uplands, where whitewashed towns and villages stand out against the deep blue sky.

Unspoiled Arcos de la Frontera tops a crag high above the Guadalete River. Wander its narrow streets, see the Moorish castle, and view the surrounding countryside.

The road continues climbing to Grazalema, known for its handwoven rugs. A detour south leads to prehistoric wall paintings in the Pileta Caves near Benaoján.

Distance and poor roads help preserve Ronda's ancient flavor. Remote and enchanting, it was first inhabited by Celts, followed by Greeks, Romans, and Moors. Three venerable bridges span the deep gorge separating the Moorish section from the newer Christian town. Modern bullfighting was born here in 1785, and Ronda has Spain's oldest bullring. The town has long attracted artists and writers, among them Goya and Hemingway.

The Costa del Sol

Once-sleepy villages and untrampled white sand beaches are now the Mediterranean playground of international sun-seekers, bronzed bodies who lounge on the sand and under bright umbrellas by day and party by night. You can enjoy the passing parade from a sidewalk cafe.

High-rise hotels and apartments loom above the beaches in the major resort areas, such as Torremolinos. But despite the bohemian popularity of the Costa del Sol, you can still find relatively uncrowded beaches

along its 106-mile coastline between Estepona and Motril.

The lively garden city of Málaga lies in the heart of the sunshine coast, mountain-sheltered from northern winds. Flowers grow luxuriantly in its mild climate. For fine views over the city and port, climb to the old Moorish castle and lovely gardens of the Alcazaba.

North to Granada

The hideaway town of Antequera, with its fine old buildings and prehistoric dolmens, is an interesting stop on the route to Granada. The road climbs eastward to the Moorish village of Archidona and on to Loja, with its narrow winding streets and Moorish fortress.

Granada is situated at the head of a valley, where the Sierra Nevada forms a snowy backdrop against blue sky. Dominating the city is the ochre red Alhambra, last stronghold of Arab rule in Spain, an enchanted world of luxuriant gardens and ornate, arcaded Moorish palaces. On a nearby hill stands a white, intimately proportioned palace with romantic gardens. It is the Generalife, summer residence of the caliphs.

South of Granada rise the slopes of the Sierra Nevada, once crossed only by mule paths but now boasting one of Europe's magnificent mountain roads. To the north are other Andalusian cities worth a visit—dignified Jaén, gracious Baeza, and the Renaissance town of Ubeda.

Historic Córdoba became a Roman town around 150 B.C., but its culture blossomed between the 8th and 11th centuries A. D. when it was the capital of Islamic Spain and the home of the caliphs. Córdoba's uniquely beautiful mosque reflects this period; centuries later, a graceful Gothic cathedral was built in the heart of the mosque. Stroll through Córdoba's narrow streets and secluded plazas to discover the city's charm—flowers cascading over whitewashed walls and wrought iron balconies, Roman and Arab ruins, shady arcades, and varied museums (one features a section on bullfighting).

Galicia's unspoiled shores

You swim in waters where Drake's ships sailed

Far from most of the country's tourist centers, the *Rías Bajas* cut deeply into the Atlantic coastline of Spain's northwestern corner. Four narrow fjord-like estuaries carve out a spectacular array of inlets and harbors, beaches and coves, crags and promontories.

Unconquered by the Moors, Galicia is a land rich in culture and history. Strong Celtic influences dominate the region, which has its own ancient lyrical language. Julius Caesar stopped at Bayona in 62 B.C. on his way to Britain, and in 1493 this small town became the first settlement to learn of America's existence. Offshore waters still conceal 18th century galleons filled with treasures from the New World, scuttled here during a battle with the English fleet.

Modern cities and scattered whitewashed villages border the unspoiled *rías*; inland, the Pontevedra countryside is etched by rivers and sprinkled with old country houses, barns on pilings, and megalithic monuments.

Rail and bus routes link the region's main towns, but you'll see much more if you have a car. Visitors without transportation will find Vigo the best center. Bayona's parador occupies a striking setting overlooking the sea.

The holy city of Santiago de Compostela makes a fine day excursion; further afield, you can explore the walled city of Lugo or head north to La Coruña.

Waterside diversions

Dominating the climate, life, and activities of the entire region is the sea. You'll find towns and seafarers' hamlets to explore and plenty of swimming beaches and picnic sites beneath the pine trees.

Each of the *rías* possesses its own special charm. The northernmost of the four, Ría de Muros y Noya, has smooth beaches and coves and is surrounded by gently undulating hills. Ría de Arosa has such diverse shoreline features that it has been compared to a miniature ocean. The firth of Pontevedra has dazzling, panoramic views, and its shores are sprinkled with small white villages.

The legendary Cies Islands, hideout and refuge for raiders and fugitives, guard the entrance to romantic Ría de Vigo. Beneath these waters lie the remains of ships loaded with gold, silver, and precious woods, sunk on their return from the West Indies to avoid surrendering them to the English.

Few towns have a more beautiful setting than the port of Vigo, which Sir Francis Drake captured and plundered more than 250 years ago. Its busy harbor is a regular port of call for ocean liners. Though a modern city, its old section holds special charm, particularly the El Berbés quarter with its flavor of the sea.

Pontevedra exudes a meditative and aristocratic air; the old monument city dates back to Roman times. To the northwest a corniche road passes Poyo monastery and follows the shore to the island resort of La Toja.

During the Middle Ages, pilgrims came to Santiago de Compostela from all over Europe to visit the tomb of St. James the Apostle. His feast day on July 25 signals a week-long city celebration. You'll find most of the town's important buildings, including the magnificent Spanish Romanesque cathedral, facing the Plaza de Obradoiro.

A sandy beach, good swimming, and a campground attract many families to the Playa de Samil, west of Vigo.

The sunny coast of Spain

Orange groves, rice fields, and resorts beside the sea

One of the sunniest regions in sunny Spain, the southeastern coast is a magnet for sun worshippers. Valencia's mild climate encourages residents and visitors alike to lead an active life outdoors near the Costa del Azahar. Farther south, you can lie on the sandy beaches of the Costa Blanca throughout the winter. Only the hardiest of sunbathers, though, can tolerate the blistering temperatures of July and August.

A fine new highway follows the coast south from the French border to Jávea. Ample accommodations exist in the coastal cities and resorts, and you'll find modern paradores beside the water of El Saler and Jávea.

The sunshine coast

Bustling Valencia sits near the sea, surrounded by a wide, fertile plain known as the *Huerta*. Many travelers time their visits to coincide with one of the city's colorful fiestas.

Though Valencia is a large and modern commercial city, its rural origins are much in evidence. Families farm the market gardens covering the densely-populated Huerta. Lush orange and lemon groves and mulberry trees delight the eye. Rice fields stretch out along the coast, providing the main ingredient of the famous *paella valenciana*, found on the menus of local restaurants.

Drive south from Valencia to the Albufera lagoon, a great freshwater lake rimmed with pines and rice fields. Only a thin sandy strip of land separates the lagoon from the sea, and you'll find camping sites and bathing beaches here among the pines. You can visit small fishing villages that border the lake (Palmar is one), go boating, or watch the waterfowl on the lagoon.

Dense orange groves extend south along the coast to Alcira, Gandia, and Oliva. Their shiny evergreen foliage, splashed with white blossoms in spring and red-gold fruit in winter, is a feast for the eyes. At night waves of perfume from the blossoms can be almost overpowering, and the fruit shines silver in the moonlight.

Inland, the most interesting town is Jativa, about 35 miles south of Valencia, the home of the Borja family. The castle of this aristocratic family—better known by the Italian form of their name, Borgia—perches on the slopes above town.

Fishermen *set their nets in the shallow, reed-filled waters of the Albufera lagoon, south of Valencia.*

Below Jávea, a great spur juts eastward into the Mediterranean. You drive south along the gentle coast from Valencia, turn the corner, and find yourself in a different land. Within a few miles the scenery changes from orange trees and rice fields to palms, olive groves, and vineyards. Tawny hills and golden-white beaches mark the beginning of the Costa Blanca. Dazzling light bathes this popular stretch of coast between Denia and Alicante. A sun-lovers' paradise, the coast is one continuous year-round resort, with Benidorm the most popular of the beaches.

Like many Spanish towns, Alicante's castle dominates the view. Date palms and roses line the wide mosaic promenade rimming the harbor. Ships sail regularly to the Balearic Islands and Algiers. Below Alicante in Moorish-looking Elche is the only palm forest in Europe. Planted by the Moors for dates, it provides all of Spain with fronds used in Palm Sunday processions.

Iberian hospitality at its best

Seek out the comfortable tourist inns of Spain and Portugal

Few Spanish hotels can match the setting of Granada's *parador*, where you stay within the mighty walls of the exotic Alhambra, as did Moorish princes and generals 700 years ago. A pebbled, patterned walkway leads through Spanish gardens to the 16th-century convent. Your cool room, decorated in Granadian style, opens onto the fountained cloister.

In the Portuguese medieval town of Óbidos, the *pousada* is located in the restored castle. The concierge leads you to your room, furnished in antiques, in the castle's watch tower. You look out on the town's crenelated walls or over gardens where flowers cascade from stairways and balconies. In the evenings you dine by candlelight in the vaulted dining room.

These are only two of the possibilities for travelers who seek out the government-operated tourist inns scattered across Spain and Portugal. Many an experienced planner plots his itinerary (and reserves well in advance) with an eye on the locations of these pleasant, moderately priced *pousadas* and *paradores*.

Portugal now has 20 *pousadas* dotting the country, while in Spain, the Ministry of Tourism operates more than 80 *paradores* (country hotels), as well as a number of *albergues* (wayside inns), *hosterias* (typical restaurants), and *refugios* (mountain shelters).

Some of the inns are located in restored historic buildings. Though fitted with modern conveniences, they retain their original character and atmosphere. Other buildings are newly constructed, built in the regional style. Prices are government controlled, depending on the degree of comfort in each inn.

The pousadas of Portugal

The first Portuguese pousada (the word comes from the idea of *repose* or *rest place*) was founded in the 12th century by a Portuguese queen. It offered pilgrims and travelers "a roof, a bed, and a candle." Today, although accommodations are much more generous, the warm hospitality continues.

These state inns, operated on a non-profit basis by the Portuguese Tourist Organization, are located both in towns and in the countryside. Similar privately-owned inns are also available, especially in resort areas.

To maintain the welcoming atmosphere of a private home where guests are received as friends, the pousadas have relatively few rooms: the largest has 28, the smallest 5 rooms. Since the pousadas are also popular with the Portuguese, it is wise to make advance reservations regardless of the season.

Inns are furnished in Portuguese style, and local food specialties are often on the menu. You can stop for a meal even if you don't plan to spend the night.

If restored historic buildings attract you, seek out the pousadas in Évora (a 14th-century monastery), Óbidos (in the castle), or on Berlenga Island (in an old fortress).

Perched atop a cliff, *the Pousada do Infante at Sagres on Portugal's southwestern tip looks out toward the sea.*

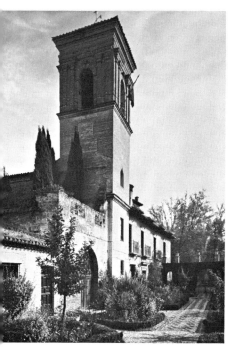

In Spain, Granada's parador (left) stands within the walled Alhambra; its dining room (center) is furnished in Andalusian style. Many of the paradores are found in restored palaces, monasteries, and castles, including this one at Oropesa, southwest of Madrid (top). On the Mediterranean coast, the Jávea parador has a beachfront location (right).

Newer pousadas offer such panoramic views as Sagres' clifftop perch above the sea, Portuguese fishing boats gliding across the lagoon of Aveiro past the Pousada da Ria, or vineyards surrounding the town of Alijó, source of the famed Port wine.

Don't expect resort-type activity and entertainment in the pousadas. They're restful, informal places where you can relax after a day's drive. Don't even plan on a hot bath the minute you step from your car, for hot water may not be available until evening. Most men wear a coat and tie for dinner, but elaborate dress certainly isn't necessary.

Spain's tourist inns

A similar network of tourist inns is found in Spain and the Canary Islands, operated by the Spanish Ministry of Tourism. Numerous new paradores have been built in the major tourist areas where accommodations have been needed.

In Spain, too, a number of historic buildings have been converted into state-run paradores, among them old palaces in Santillana del Mar (see page 117), Avila (see page 119), Oropesa and Jarandilla, west of Madrid, and Alarcón, on the Madrid-Valencia route.

Near the Portuguese border you can stay in the 14th-century castle of King Henry II in Ciudad Rodrigo, in an old convent in the center of Mérida, and in an ancient castle in Zafra.

In Andalusia, unusual parador accommodations are available inside Granada's Alhambra, at the cavernous Castillo Santa Catalina in Jaén, and in a 16th-century Renaissance palace at Ubeda, north of Jaén.

Motorists in transit can take advantage of the *albergues*, wayside inns along Spain's major highways, in which the weary traveler can find a good meal and a comfortable bed, as well as a garage and gasoline at any hour of the day or night. Sportsmen can seek out mountain paradores or the simpler *refugios* as headquarters for fishing, hunting, or mountaineering.

Mediterranean furnishings predominate in the inns. Your room may have a grillwork balcony and a pleasant view, or perhaps there'll be a quiet garden where you can unwind. Recently-built inns often have air conditioning and a swimming pool; paradores in resort areas may have sports facilities nearby.

Information and reservations

A list of pousadas with a current price schedule can be obtained by writing to the Casa de Portugal (address on page 131). Reservations are made directly with each pousada; travelers are limited to a stay of five days in each inn.

The Spanish National Tourist Office (address on page 131) provides information on its state-operated inns and restaurants. Travelers can stay a maximum of 10 days at each parador and albergue during the tourist season; longer stays are permitted in winter. Reservations are made individually with each inn.

WHERE TRADITIONAL CRAFTS ENDURE

In your readings and travels, you've undoubtedly become aware of the wide array of hand-made products still fashioned by European craftsmen, using traditional skills which have been passed down for generations from father to son.

Many of the crafts are mentioned elsewhere in this book—ranging from the copper cookware of Normandy to hand-carved violins in the Bavarian Alps, from the pottery villages of Portugal to Swedish glassware towns. You'll find a number of touring and shopping suggestions listed in the index under *Handicrafts*.

A country's hand-made products reflect a facet of the people and their way of life, and the items often provide lasting and useful mementoes of your trips. Sometimes you can watch craftsmen at work. You'll reawaken memories each time you use Christmas ornaments or a colorful pottery bowl.

How to find the craft areas. If you're interested in learning more about a country's crafts, and possibly visiting a workshop or two, how do you find them?

In your preliminary travel reading, make notes on craft specialties that interest you, jotting down the town or region where the craft predominates. Some basic guidebooks devote chapters to regional crafts; your local library is a good place to start. Don't neglect special interest books and publications; craft magazines often present ideas or new trends from abroad.

Government tourist information offices may have brochures detailing their country's crafts. Request any information they have, including workshops open to visitors or shops specializing in handicrafts. Several countries have government-sponsored stores that assemble and sell the best of the country's regional handicrafts. The tourist office may be able to provide addresses of rural craft cooperatives.

Ask friends who have traveled for suggestions on places they may have discovered during their own wanderings.

On-the-spot searching. Once you're in Europe, keep alert. Nearly every large town (and many smaller ones as well) have stores specializing in the crafts of the country. Needless to say, quality ranges from excellent to indifferent.

Many rural markets and fairs have crafts of the region on display; sometimes craft demonstrations are in progress. If you're in doubt about the price, have the seller write it down. In country towns you will often see objects made locally on display in shop windows or in actual use in hotels and restaurants.

Local tourist offices usually know if any local artisans welcome visitors. Even if you have difficulty overcoming the language barrier, working demonstrations are well worth watching. Often samples of the work will be available for sale in an adjoining shop. If you don't have room in your luggage to hand-carry items, inquire about shipping before making your purchase, remembering that most small shops have limited packing and shipping facilities. Breakable objects need careful packing, and you'd be wise to ask about breakage insurance and replacement.

What to look for. Handicrafts vary from country to country, depending on practical needs of the people, available raw materials, and traditional skills. Many of the best craft regions thrive where winter weather or isolation limits contacts.

Hand-crafted articles cover a wide range, including pottery and ceramics, glassware, jewelry and metalwork, wood carving, raffia and wickerwork, hand-woven textiles, rugs and tapestries, lace and embroidery, leatherwork, toys, and Christmas ornaments.

Craftsmen still pursue traditional skills: (left to right) *a Romanian potter trains an apprentice; a wood-carver fashions wooden shoes in a Dutch marketplace; a glass-blower shapes a bottle in Biot, France.*

Wine touring in Portugal

Visit vineyards and pottery towns on a loop from Oporto

Portugal's wine country comes alive in autumn, when families from remote mountain villages make their way to the terraced vineyards above the Douro valley for the annual grape harvest. The country's finest wine region lies east of Oporto in northern Portugal. Here you'll find vineyards yielding the unique *vinho verde* (green wine) and, in the upper Douro, the famous Port.

During the annual harvest (beginning in mid-September and lasting through October), women cut the grape bunches from the vines, filling large baskets that men carry on their backs down the slopes. Musicians accompany the workers to and from the vineyards and during nighttime dancing and partying.

Casks of wine are shipped downriver by rail or on the traditional *rabelos*, the high-prowed, flat-bottomed, square-rigged Douro riverboats, steered with poles and rudder. Brought to the old, dimly-lit warehouses of Vila Nova de Gaia (see page 131), the wine ages slowly until ready for shipping.

Up the Douro valley

A good road follows the Douro upriver from Oporto, winding between undulating hills. Flowers brighten the roadsides. White houses and villages stand out against the green slopes. Beneath family grape arbors, corn and beans often grow. Soon vineyards appear between the terraced olive orchards and corn fields. Near Entre-os-Rios, the green valley of the Tâmega river angles northwest toward Amarante.

Commercial center for the light and sparkling, fruity *vinho verde* wine is Sinfães. Port-producing vineyards begin near Régua, extending eastward along the Douro to the Spanish border.

Vila Real and Amarante are busy small towns with attractive Renaissance houses. Look in Vila Real shops for examples of the region's distinctive black pottery. Just outside town is the elegant Mateus manor *(solar)*, with gardens and orchards, a lake, and vineyards producing Mateus rosé wine.

Amarante's houses ascend a slope above the tree-shaded Tâmega River. A local agricultural center, Ama-

rante hosts one of Portugal's most colorful fairs on the first Saturday in June. In the town hall a small museum displays works of local Cubist painter Amadeu de Sousa Cardoso.

Accommodations are limited in the small towns, but you'll find *pousadas* (see page 124) in Alijó in the vineyards and at São Gonçalo, east of Amarante.

If time permits, add a northern loop into the province of Minho, known for its colorful fairs and festivals. Unspoiled Guimarães, first capital of the kingdom of Portugal, contains a classical old quarter and a ducal castle with rich tapestries. Craftsmen sell their wares each Tuesday at the Braga fairgrounds, and Thursday is market day in the pottery town of Barcelos. You reach the coast at Esposende and return to Oporto through the coastal lacemaking communities of Póvoa de Varzim, Vila do Conde, and Azurara.

Terraced vineyards *and scattered white houses cover the undulating hills above the Douro River near Regua.*

A Portuguese sampler

Fishing ports and fortress towns delight you

The restful countryside of Portugal delights travelers previously familiar only with its large cities and resorts. Once you're out of Lisbon, traffic is pleasantly light, except in larger towns. Roads are often lined with greenery and are usually paved, though they sometimes become narrow and twisting passing through villages.

One small town after another tempts you to stop. Sturdy castles and protective ramparts are constant reminders of centuries of warfare and domination. White-washed houses, adorned with black wrought-iron grills and splashed with flowers, cluster below each fortress.

Along the coast, windmills give off a humming noise as their sails rotate in the wind, and waterwheels are set spinning by power from inland rivers and streams.

Crafts flourish in many small towns; you'll see them displayed in outdoor markets and fairs, as well as in shops and regional museums. Colorful glazed tiles (called *azulejos*) ornament many churches, public buildings, and patrician homes.

In walled Óbidos, you can stay in the pousada in the castle and walk along the ramparts surrounding the town.

The central coast

Once you've seen the sights of Lisbon and made the triangle trip to Estoril, Cascais, and Sintra, it's time to sample the Portuguese countryside.

About 60 miles north of Lisbon, crenelated walls enclose the enchanting medieval town of Óbidos. Bright geraniums and bougainvillea cascade from stairways and balconies of dazzling white houses. Donkeys and pedestrians have the right-of-way in streets barely wide enough for a single car. A *pousada* is located in the castle (see page 124). You can walk along parts of the city wall.

West of Óbidos, the fishing port of Peniche is a scene of great activity when the fishing boats unload their catch, and there's a boisterous market on the quay.

From Peniche daily boat service leaves for Berlenga Island, an ancient fortress lying off the coast. You can walk shoreline paths, go fishing, make a boat trip along the cave-hollowed coast, or try skin diving (arrange for equipment in Peniche). A pousada in the fortress is open from June through September.

Another favorite fishing village is Nazaré, with its wide sandy beach and colorful fishing fleet. On this harborless coast, fishermen must roll their boats down the beach over logs and launch them against the incoming waves. Returning boats are pulled high on the beach by hand, or by teams of Nazaré oxen.

Inland in a region of fruit orchards and small pottery towns lies Alcobaça. Ornate tombs, including that of Portuguese king Dom Pedro, are found in the monastery.

Elaborate monasteries and craft towns

Some of Portugal's most innovative architecture dates from the early 16th century reign of Manuel I. One of the best places to see its details is the Batalha monastery. In the building, parts of which remain unfinished, Gothic simplicity is enhanced with such Manueline details as tracery, carved marble arcades, and decorated columns.

As in many Portuguese towns, a historic castle dominates Leiria. Here you'll probably see displays of crafts from neighboring villages—glassware and pottery, woven bedspreads and basketware.

Flamboyant architecture of the Batalha echoes the wealth of the Manueline era (left). Portuguese fish markets display an intriguing variety of fish and shellfish (top). High-prowed boats are pulled up on the sandy beach at Nazaré (center). Slender colonnades of the Roman temple of Diana stand just outside the pousada at Évora (right).

Great crowds of fervent pilgrims visit the shrine of Fátima, particularly on the 13th of the month (largest pilgrimages occur on May 12-13 and October 12-13). Many travel on foot to the shrine, some covering the final distance to the Basilica on their knees.

Another interesting site is Tomar, where the Church of the Templars reveals Manueline decoration carried to extravagance. The town's Tabuleiros festival, held in July during even numbered years, attracts many visitors. In Abrantes, flower-filled alleyways lead up to the fortress ruins, where you have a view over the Tagus valley.

Sampling the vast Alentejo

Access to Marvão is difficult, but you'll be glad you made the effort. Anchored atop a granite peak near the Spanish border, the town is a delight, and there's a pousada if you want to stay overnight. Narrow alleys lace the small town below the fortress. From atop the still-intact ramparts, you look down on the town, across to Spain's jagged mountains, and over the vast Alentejo plain.

In nearby Portalegre you can make weekday visits to the tapestry workshop, located in the former monastery, to see hand-woven tapestries made and displayed.

Stretching southward is the flat Alentejo plain, its large grain fields occasionally broken by cork oak trees or a herd of grazing bulls. In the Alentejo pottery center of Estremoz, wares are arrayed on the main square at the Saturday market, near the small regional museum.

Allow a full day to explore Évora, one of Portugal's most colorful cities and the market center of the Alentejo. A walled town since the Roman era, Évora now exudes a Moorish flavor with its arched alleyways, daz-

zling-white houses, balconies, and hanging gardens.

The town flourished under the Romans, declined under the Visigoths, and in 715 was occupied by the Moors. From its rich past it retains a Roman temple and many handsome medieval and Renaissance buildings. An aqueduct winds through undulating countryside, bringing water to the city.

Arraiolos is known for its brilliantly colored wool carpets, executed in simple designs.

South of Lisbon

As you return to the coast, the landscape becomes greener. Scattered olive trees, rice fields, and vineyards come in view as you approach Setúbal.

This busy port facing the wide Sado estuary is a prosperous industrial center, particularly since completion of the bridge from Lisbon across the Tagus. Its fishing fleet numbers more than 2,000 boats, and you may detect the pungent aroma of sardines coming from large canneries near the docks.

Sesimbra's clear waters are a favorite of underwater fishermen and swimmers. In this sunny little resort, washing hangs out the windows, and sometimes you'll even see fish hung from doorways and windows to dry. Try to plan your visit for late afternoon, when the fleet returns and the catch is auctioned on the beach.

On weekdays you can visit the Bacalhoa *quinta*, a large Portuguese country estate near the Lisbon-Setúbal road. Its architecture shows Moorish and Florentine influences, rather than the fanciful Manueline style. Pictorial *azulejos* face the garden pavilion, and you'll enjoy a stroll through the quiet gardens.

Portugal's garden coast

The Moors left their mark along the Algarve shore

An exotic Moorish flavor tinges Portugal's sunny southern coast. Blinding-white towns face south toward Africa, their flat-roofed buildings and tall lacy chimneys outlined against the Algarve's brilliant blue sky.

Warm temperatures and wide, golden beaches lure sun-lovers, while in the coastal hills the region is one vast subtropical garden. Flowers bloom prolifically in the glinting sun. Climbing the gentle slopes are huge orchards of fig and apricot trees, olive and orange groves, carob and cork trees. In January, almond trees burst into bloom, veiling the landscape in snowy splendour.

It's a day's drive from Lisbon to the Algarve coast or a 35-minute flight from the capital to Faro. Threading the region's main towns, the main highway wends east from the Sagres peninsula to the Spanish border. Spur roads lead down from the main road to resorts and the sea.

Capital of the Algarve is bustling and colorful Faro. City life revolves around the busy harbor area, but you'll also enjoy the pleasantly shaded city gardens, the peaceful old quarter, and the patterned mosaic pavements and shops along the Rua Santo António.

To the east lie small towns so Moorish in appearance you could easily imagine yourself in North Africa: Olhão, with its narrow alleys, white cube-shaped houses, and lively fish market; Fuseta and its good beach; and Tavira, a town of flat roofs and weird chimneys and minarets. Tuna fishing is a busy summer industry here.

Pine trees border Monte Gordo's sandy beach. From the ancient fortified castle of Castro Marim, you gaze across the border to Spain.

West of Faro lie the major resorts: lively Albufeira, the fishing port of Portimão, celebrated Praia da Rocha, and Lagos, situated on its magnificent bay. Among smaller hideaways are elegant Vale do Lobo and the fishing villages of Quarteria and Armação de Pêra. All along the coast, sandy beaches nestle beneath reddish-brown cliffs, inviting swimmers and sunbathers.

Beyond Lagos, you enter the windswept Sagres peninsula, haunted by the spirit of Prince Henry the Navigator, who lived on this lonely outpost in the 15th century, dreaming of finding a sea route to the riches of India. His old navigation school, buffeted by unceasing Atlantic gales, still stands on the bleak headland; try to plan your visit to see the movie shown there (an English version is shown daily at 3:45 P.M.).

Inland excursions

For a different glimpse of the Algarve, drive inland. Estói has a fine 18-century palace and formal gardens. The market town and craft center of Loulé is renowned for the varied collection of openwork chimneys atop its white houses. Continue toward Silves, one of Portugal's oldest cities. East of town stop for a look at the unusual Portuguese cross, then tour the ancient Arab castle and its huge underground cisterns.

North from Silves or Portimão you drive up an orchard-covered valley into the mountains. The road climbs beneath eucalyptus and pines up the slopes of the Fóia, highest point in the range, to a viewpoint with superb vistas over southwestern Portugal.

Beaching boats is a team effort along the Algarve shore. Logs are used as rollers to help move the boat across the sand.

IN SPAIN AND PORTUGAL: special interests

ISLAND TRIPS ● If you want a change of pace from mainland sightseeing, several island retreats are within easy reach of the Iberian Peninsula by air or sea.

Three hundred miles west of the Portuguese coast are the Azores, for many years merely a port of call but now a "new" destination for travelers who think Europe holds no more surprises. The Azores' volcanic origin is reflected in the rugged coastline, but the island's unspoiled natural beauty of fertile fields, luxuriant flowers, and mountain lakes incorporates many of the Continent's most scenic features. Santa Maria and Terceira are the main islands.

Southeast from Lisbon is Madeira, a year-round resort known for its pleasant climate and lush vegetation. Bullock sled is the traditional way to see the town of Funchal, or you may prefer to spend your visit roaming the city on foot or shopping for Madeira lace or basketware.

You can continue south to the Canary Islands, a favorite resort for many vacationing Europeans some 650 miles below Europe's southernmost tip. Though under the Spanish government, the seven islands exist in a separate world. Major islands are Tenerife and Gran Canaria. The western islands are lush and humid, those near Africa drier and hotter. Inter-island plane and boat service is frequent. Each island has a parador, in addition to other accommodations.

Off Spain's Mediterranean coast are the sun-drenched Balearic Islands, each providing a different atmosphere. Largest of the isles is Majorca, where a sociable resort atmosphere prevails. For a quieter spot, try green Minorca or hot Ibiza. Adventurous travelers find Formentera simple and inexpensive. You can fly to Palma de Mallorca from many European cities, or travel by boat from Barcelona, Valencia, and Alicante.

DON QUIXOTE'S LA MANCHA ● Aficionados of Cervantes have reconstructed the routes across sunbaked, central Spain followed by his idealistic fictional hero, Don Quixote, and his faithful squire, Sancho Panza. Several places linked with Cervantes' tales can be found east of Toledo and Ciudad Real: the home town of Quixote, Argamasilla de Alba; Campo de Criptana, where he battled the windmills; and El Toboso, home of his lady-love, Dulcinea.

WHERE TO HEAR THE FADO ● The nostalgic side of the Portuguese character comes forth in the *fados*, those sad and monotonous chants denouncing human passions and the forces of destiny. In Lisbon, *fado* can be heard in restaurants in the older parts of town—the Alfama, the Mouraria, and the Bairro Alto. The singer, often a woman, is accompanied by one or more guitar players.

In Coimbra the *fado* is livelier in melody, often with sentimental themes. Here it is traditionally sung by the university students, who stand in the streets to serenade the town's prettiest girls. (The tattered hems of the students' black capes reflect a romantic custom; when a young lady gives a student a kiss, she is rewarded with a piece of cloth from the bottom of his robe.)

PORT AND SHERRY ● During your visit to the Iberian Peninsula, you might like to sample Portugal's port and Spain's sherry in the wineries.

Oporto, in the north of Portugal, is home of the famous port wine. From the eastern mountains, wine is brought down the Douro River to wine lodges in the city's Vila Nova de Gaia quarter on the river's south bank. Visitors are welcome on weekdays.

Jerez de la Frontera, south of Seville, is Spain's sherry capital. Vineyards surround the town, and visitors are welcomed at *bodegas* to tour and sample the three different types of sherries. During the second week of September, Jerez celebrates with a vintage festival.

CHILDREN'S PORTUGAL ● Miniature models of Portuguese houses and major monuments are displayed at Coimbra's *Portugal dos Pequinitos*. A children's zoo and playground are also on the park grounds.

DINING IN SPAIN ● Meal hours are much later in Spain than in other Western countries, and some travelers have difficulty adjusting to them.

Lunch is served from 1:30 P.M. on; in Madrid 2:30 is a normal lunch hour, and 3 or 3:30 P.M. is not uncommon. Few restaurants serve dinner before 9 P.M.; the usual dinner hour is 10 P.M., though in Madrid and the south, the hour is often 10:30 or 11 P.M.

If you find it difficult to last until mealtime, find a cafe and select from a variety of tempting hot and cold snacks, called *tapas*. Seafood and meat, open-faced sandwiches, and sausages can be paired with beer or a glass of white wine to stave off hunger.

Information on some of Spain's regional food specialties and wines is available in a booklet issued by the Spanish National Tourist Office.

HANDICRAFTS ● Shoppers will find an intriguing array of handicrafts, including many regional specialties.

Among Spanish handicrafts are leatherwork, jewelry, furniture, pottery, embroidery and lace, and metalwork. Spain's official handicraft shop is a good starting point: Artesania Espanola, Floridablanca 1, Madrid.

Regional crafts in Portugal include filigree work, ceramics, embroidery and lace, rugs and quilts, wooden articles, and wickerwork. Handicrafts from throughout Portugal are on display in Lisbon's Museum of Popular Art near the Belém Tower (open daily except Mondays and holidays).

Spanish National Tourist Offices
665 Fifth Avenue, New York, N.Y. 10022
180 North Michigan Avenue, Chicago, Ill. 60601
209 Post Street, San Francisco, Calif. 94108
338 Biscayne Boulevard, Miami, Florida 33132
Casa del Hidalgo, St. Augustine, Florida 32084

Portuguese National Tourist Offices
548 Fifth Avenue, New York, N.Y. 10036
17 East Monroe Street, Suite 500, Chicago, Ill. 60690
3250 Wilshire Boulevard, Los Angeles, Calif. 90010

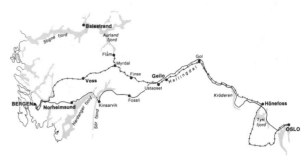

Over the top of Norway to Bergen

By road or rail—farmland, forests, icy mountains, fjords

Several scenic routes link Norway's two largest cities— Oslo and Bergen—but none offers more awesome countryside than the way through the Hallingdal valley and across the Hardanger mountain plateau.

Both the "Reindeer Road" and the Bergen Railway follow routes through this ever-changing countryside. They wend from agricultural valleys through pine forests up into the bleak, icy mountains, then dip into western Norway's beautiful fjord country. The rail line operates year round, but the road across the Hardanger plateau is open only from late May to November.

The Bergen Railway

During the fascinating 8½-hour rail trip from Oslo to Bergen, you sample Norway's varying lands. Completed in 1909 and completely electrified, the railroad is an

engineering feat. It has more than 60 miles of track above timberline in country covered by snow most of the year. Passing waterfalls and glaciers, trains go through about 200 tunnels and 18 miles of snow sheds on their way from Oslo fjord to the North Atlantic. Many of Norway's famous ski resorts are located along the rail line; skiing lasts from Christmas through April at most resorts.

Leaving Oslo, the train heads for the lakes, woods, and hills of Nordmarka, where residents of Oslo go on country outings. Later you pass through the Hallingdal district, where Norwegian peasant culture still survives.

West of Geilo, one of Norway's largest resorts, the railroad enters the high mountain zone, crossing near the base of Hallingskarvet, an impressive mountain wall 21 miles long. Near Finse the almost circular Hardangerjökul glacier comes into view. High snow fences and covered snow sheds shield the tracks from the worst of the weather, a necessity at this elevation (4,300 feet). Many farms here have tall storehouses for winter provisions, and some buildings have sod roofs.

If you are alert, just before Myrdal you'll see one of the trip's best sights: a view down more than 1,000 feet to the Flåmsdal below, a huge ravine yawning at the foot of towering mountains.

West of Voss the train enters fjord country, giving you glimpses of some of Europe's most spectacular scenery between the numerous railway tunnels.

To Bergen by boat

If you'd like to prolong your journey to Bergen another day, get off the train in Myrdal. This way you can combine a ride on the unique Flåm rail line with a fjord trip into Bergen.

In Myrdal, you entrain again on one of the world's steepest railways, descending to the town of Flåm on Aurland fjord. This 13-mile branch line drops 2,800 feet, runs through 21 tunnels, and completes a circle inside a mountain tunnel to reach the valley. Emerging from the tunnel, the train crosses the thundering Kjosfoss Falls (stopping so that passengers can take photographs) and

Myrdal, dwarfed by surrounding mountains, is departure point for the Flåm line, which drops steeply to a fjord.

Fyksesund Bridge spans the Hardanger fjord near the village of Norheimsund, east of Bergen (left). May is blossom time in the fjord country; orchards of fruit trees along the Hardanger fjord and the Sör fjord burst into a frothy sea of pink and white blossoms (right).

continues down the valley to the village at the edge of the fjord. After spending the night in Flåm, the next day you continue by ferry to Bergen (changing ships in midfjord) along the beautiful Sogne fjord—a spectacular climax for your journey.

The meshing of boat and train connections allows travelers going from west to east (Bergen to Oslo) to make the fjord excursion from Bergen to Flåm, take the rail trip up to Myrdal, and still catch a late afternoon train into Oslo all on the same day.

Driving in Norway

Even if you wanted to hurry along Norway's roads, it wouldn't be possible. Roads skirt the sides of mountains, drop through narrow crevasses, tunnel through towering cliffs of ice, zigzag in hairpin turns down rocky cliffsides, and inevitably lead to a ferry or bridge that crosses a fjord. Although roads are frequently narrow and usually graveled, they are well maintained and certainly safe enough for the careful driver.

From June to October, the mountain passes are free of snow, the weather is mild, and Norway's northern latitude affords extra daylight hours (during June and July, daylight never completely fades, even at midnight). Roadside inns and tourist hotels are located at the edges of glaciers or on the shores of lakes in the high mountain country. Permanent camp sites, where you can pitch your tent for a small fee, are spaced every few miles along the main routes.

Along the "Reindeer Road"

From Oslo the 317-mile "Reindeer Road" climbs into the Hallingdal valley, crosses the high Hardanger plateau, and descends the awesome Måbödal valley to the fjord country. Allow three days for the automobile trip.

You skirt the Oslo fjord to Sandvika, then gradually ascend through gentle hills and dense woods to Skaret.

Stop here for a view over Lake Tyrifjord and Ringerike, with Norefjell in the background. At Sundvollen you can ride a chair lift to the summit of Krokkleiva, then continue on to Hönefoss, where a large waterfall runs through the middle of the town. Around Lake Kröderen, hilly country and little farms push down to the wooded shores of the lake. At Nesbyen, visiting the Museum of Valley Folk Art can be a pleasant break.

Beyond Gol the road follows broad rapids that churn over enormous rocks in the Hallingdal River. At Torpo, about 10 miles west of Gol, is one of Norway's famous stave churches. The main road continues to the resorts of Geilo and Ustaoset.

West of Geilo you enter the Hardanger mountain plateau. You cross broad tundra, scrubby and ragged, but brilliantly colored with purples and browns and flecked with yellow and crimson. Snow from the Hardangerjökul glacier blends almost indistinguishably into the low-hanging clouds above it. Here, after a 200-mile climb from Oslo, you reach the highest point on the trip.

As you start downhill, there's a breathtaking view of 620-foot Vöringsfoss waterfall. In a fast drop of about 20 miles down the awe-inspiring Måbödal valley—along hairpin turns, through tunnels, and along the edges of sheer precipices—you lose all the altitude that you had previously picked up in 200 miles of gradual climbing.

Following along, and sometimes through, the fjord walls, the road leads to Kinsarvik, on the Sör fjord. Fruit orchards line the fjord's eastern shore.

From Kinsarvik to Kvanndal, 80 miles east of Bergen, it's a 50-minute ferry boat ride. The road from Kvanndal to Bergen follows along the Hardanger fjord, crosses the 1,035-foot Fyksesund suspension bridge, then passes through orchard lands to Norheimsund, a popular holiday center on the fjord.

The last lap—to Bergen—features a charming blend of mountains, fjords, and lakes. North of Nesttun you pass near Troldhaugen, home of Edvard Grieg, and the Fantoft stave church.

Land of the Midnight Sun

You can cruise to North Cape, meet the Lapps, enjoy the outdoors

Where in Europe do you go if you feel a surge of frontier spirit? To the vast country north of the Arctic Circle—Europe's last wilderness.

Spectacular vistas of snow-capped mountains and the fjord-indented coast are punctuated by the sparkling lakes, tumbling rivers, pine and birch forests, and wild tundra of the interior. Here you can join in a host of outdoor activities or visit encampments where Lapps tend their herds of grazing reindeer.

The long day of the Midnight Sun—when the sun never sets—arrives in late May and lasts until mid-July near the Arctic Circle. On the weekend nearest Midsummer, celebrations occur all over Scandinavia.

Midsummer Night *near Bodö is celebrated with night-long bonfires, midnight picnics, dancing and singing.*

Early in September, the first frosts create a brief explosion of vibrant color inland. Trees and shrubs glow in shades of yellow and red and russet. Colors often emerge overnight and vanish a few days later.

Transportation and accommodations

Once you decide to head for the far north, a wide choice of transportation is possible. If you use only surface transportation the vast distances eat up time. Often you can combine several modes of travel to advantage.

Scandinavian Airlines and Finnair serve major cities north of the Arctic Circle, and from early June to mid-July, Scandinavian Airlines offers overnight round-trip Midnight Sun excursions from Stockholm to Kiruna for visitors who want a glimpse of the northland.

Throughout the year coastal steamers cruise north from Bergen along Norway's spectacular fjord coast, past North Cape to Kirkenes, making brief stops along the way. Rail lines head north from Stockholm via Boden and Kiruna to Narvik on the Norwegian coast, from Trondheim north to Bodö, and from Helsinki to Rovaniemi and Kemijärvi.

A system of connecting bus lines provides the best way of getting around in the far north. Local bus lines fan out from the main bus and rail routes to remote areas. If you are driving, you'll find most roads are graveled, though some are oiled. The best months for driving are from late June through September (spring thaw makes some roads impassable until mid-June).

Good tourist inns and hotels dot the towns and the main roads, and in favorite recreation areas, new hotels and holiday villages have been built. Tourist inns are not luxurious, but they are modern, clean, centrally heated, and moderately priced. In view of the region's limited accommodations and short season, you should make reservations well in advance.

Fjord route to North Cape

The majestic scenery of Norway's fjord coast has attracted travelers for years. For many visitors the impor-

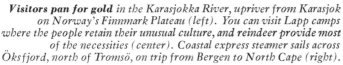
Visitors pan for gold in the Karasjokka River, upriver from Karasjok on Norway's Finnmark Plateau (left). You can visit Lapp camps where the people retain their unusual culture, and reindeer provide most of the necessities (center). Coastal express steamer sails across Öksfjord, north of Tromsö, on trip from Bergen to North Cape (right).

tant destination is North Cape, Europe's northernmost outpost, a lonely cliff rising nearly a thousand feet above the Arctic Ocean at 71° latitude.

You can make the trip by coastal steamer from Bergen along the coast or travel by bus or car on the Arctic Highway. From early June to mid-September, the "Polar Express" bus makes a four-day run from Fauske to Kirkenes, making overnight stops at Narvik, Sörkjosen, and Lakselv. If you plan to drive, allow six travel days between Trondheim and North Cape. You'll leave your car or bus at Repvåg, board a ferry to the fishing village of Honningsvåg, and continue by bus to North Cape.

A warming Gulf Stream moderates Norway's coastal climate. Narvik's ice-free port is an important shipping point, and Tromso has been the jumping-off place for expeditions into the Arctic and to the North Pole. You can see objects from these trips at the Arctic Museum, which also has a Lapp collection. Bodö and Hammerfest, both destroyed in World War II and since rebuilt, are thriving fishing ports.

Summer in Lapland

Spring appears suddenly in Lapland. In May the first flowers peek through melting snows, and rivers thunder with ice floes. From first thaw to first snowfall, Scandinavians devote nearly every spare waking hour to outdoor activities, fun that you can share.

Hikers will find a fine network of trails in the highlands and across the fells and tundra (see page 151). The season begins after Midsummer and lasts into September. Because it also explodes with insects, remember to bring insect repellent.

Fishing is excellent in Lapland's lakes and rivers and in the Swedish highlands. Guided fishing and hunting trips are available, with air taxi service to remote areas.

You can fish for salmon in several rivers or go deep-sea fishing from Hammerfest. Travelers can shoot the rapids on Norway's Alta River or in Finland's Kuusamo district, east of Rovaniemi, or make boat trips on the Tana River (see page 146) or on some of the larger lakes.

A minor gold rush started here nearly a hundred years ago, and if you like, you can still pan for gold yourself — in the Karasjokka River, 45 miles upriver from Karasjok on Norway's Finnmark Plateau, or in the remote tributaries of the Lemmenjoki and Ivalo rivers, west of Ivalo in Finland.

An interesting day trip is the train ride between Kiruna and Narvik on the scenic "iron ore route." Ore is mined in the iron mountain in Kiruna (visitors welcome June to August) and shipped by rail to the Norwegian port of Narvik. Since the railway provides the only access to some scenic areas in the highlands, a number of tourist centers have sprung up along the rail line.

Lapp villages

Stretching across the northernmost regions of Scandinavia, the wild tundra of Lapland is inhabited mainly by Lapps, a nomadic people with their own language, cultural traditions, colorful red and blue costumes, and handicrafts. Most Lapps have given up the nomadic life, but some still follow the reindeer herds.

Reindeer provide the Lapps with food, skins for warm clothing, bones and antlers for implements. Highlight of the Lapp year is the annual winter reindeer roundup.

Among the more accessible Lapp settlements are Karasjok and Kautokeino in Norway; Jokkmokk, Gällivare, and Jukkasjärvi in Sweden; Rovaniemi, Enontekio, Kilpisjärvi, Inari, and Utsjoki in Finland. Some towns have Lapp museums, tracing their history, showing how they live, and showcasing Lappish handicrafts.

Touring the Telemark district

By train, bus, and boat into scenic rural Norway

Some of Norway's most spectacular scenery is found in the Telemark district. You can visit Telemark's dense forests and pastoral farmlands from May through September, but if you plan to venture into the higher elevations, wait until June.

Ancient dwellings and local craftsmen draw you back in time. Yet you'll also see modern tourist hotels and giant power stations that harness the nation's abundant water energy.

Motorists can drive through Telemark on surfaced roads or you may prefer to travel by rail, boat, and bus, sitting back and enjoying the vistas. Local bus routes link the main valleys and villages. Pay close attention not only to the scenery but also to timetables.

Telemark costume is colorful and richly embroidered. Log cabins are common in Norway's rural settlements.

The heart of Telemark

Telemark Museum in Skien's Brekke Park provides visitors with a broad cultural overview of the region. Open from mid-May to mid-September, its collections show old architecture and native arts and crafts, such as wood carving, weaving, and silver work. Dramatist Henrik Ibsen was a native son, and you can visit the old farm near Skien where he once lived.

Approaching the heart of Telemark by boat is a delightful experience. In summer the old paddle-steamer *Victoria* makes an all-day trip from Skien up the Telemark Canal and across long finger lakes to Dalen (see page 146).

If you prefer to travel by bus from Skien, you'll skirt Lake Norsjö on your way to Bö, the transportation hub of central Telemark. Or you can reach Bö by train from Oslo. Afternoon buses take you through the Morgedal district—where modern skiing originated—on to Vrådal or Dalen before dinner. Vrådal is a quiet lake resort, Dalen is the center of the giant Tokke hydroelectric project.

If you're motoring, detour a few miles to the Heddal stave church just west of Notodden, one of Norway's largest and most beautiful stave churches (open daily in summer).

Near Rauland you can see old villages and farmsteads preserved in natural surroundings. Local craftsmen continue to work at regional crafts in time-honored ways. Scenery is spectacular in this corner of Telemark. Hiking and fishing can provide a good change of pace.

From Rauland you follow the edge of Lake Mösvatn down to Rjukan, at the foot of Mount Gausta (6,120 feet); a cable railway transports visitors up the mountain. During World War II, the Nazis produced "heavy water" here for use in atomic bomb experiments. In a daring raid, Norwegian commandos sabotaged the plant.

From Rjukan you can return via Notodden to Oslo by train (including a train-ferry trip down Lake Tinnsjö) or travel by bus around the lake and across the mountains to Kongsberg, where you continue to Oslo by rail.

Island adventure in the Baltic

Ruins and roses highlight your visit to Gotland

A journey to the sunny island of Gotland, lying in the Baltic Sea sixty miles off Sweden's eastern shore, takes you back into the medieval past and the earlier days of the Vikings. Its capital, Visby, was once the cultural crossroads for all of Scandinavia and a key city in the Hanseatic League.

Today the quiet town exudes a medieval air. Visby's magnificent city wall, built in the 12th and 13th centuries, is largely intact and surrounds the town for about 2½ miles on all but the sea side.

Walking in Visby

Visby is just the right size to explore on foot. The inner town, within the walls, is not quite a mile long and a half-mile wide. Inside the walls are 16 churches, all but one in ruins, all going back to Hanseatic days and earlier. Brilliant red roses brighten many of Visby's buildings and stone ruins.

You'll find colorful maps posted at intervals to help you find your way. Start high on the south side of town at the square called Södertorg. Then work your way across and down, eventually winding up at the harbor. Along the way, mixed in with the ruins, are shops, pensions, cafes, hotels, and tightly-built Swedish provincial houses with red tile roofs and bright flower boxes. In Strandgatan, the old main street of Hansa times, several stepped-gable houses stand, buildings that were used as stores in the 13th century.

Elsewhere on the island

Swedes come to Gotland on holiday all summer long, usually crossing over by ship. Gotland is the warmest of Sweden's provinces, the island's swimming beaches among the best in Scandinavia.

Gotland has prehistoric sites and Viking remains to visit, dozens of ruined churches, unusual limestone "rauks" shaped by the Baltic's waves, and the stalactite caves of Lummelunda. Guided trips allow you to visit the offshore island bird sanctuaries south of Visby.

In early July the Gotlanders stage their Stångaspelen —athletic games dating back to Viking times, with such events as varpa (stone disk throwing) and pole hurling. Outdoor concerts and operatic performances take place frequently in July and August, sometimes in the romantic St. Nikolaus church ruins.

Daily flights from Stockholm's Bromma Airport reach Visby in less than an hour. Or you can travel to the island's capital by car ferry from Nynäshamn, Oskarshamn, Västervik, or Oxelösund.

Visby's accommodations range from comfortable hotels to inexpensive pensions and seaside guest houses near the swimming beaches. Simple lodging is available in the island's main towns. Since Gotland is a popular holiday destination, make arrangements in advance for a summer visit.

City wall *of Visby surrounds the town. The island has dozens of medieval churches, most of them in ruins.*

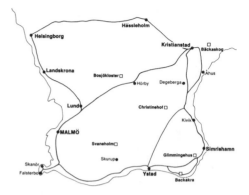

Sweden's château country

Sunny seaside resorts have been touched by history

What the Riviera is to France, Skåne is to Sweden. From June through September, this small but prosperous province of fertile farmland edged with sandy beaches becomes Sweden's vacation land. Situated on Sweden's southern tip, Skåne is "château country," where more than 150 castles and manor houses dot the gentle, rolling countryside.

Sweden's southern provinces belonged to Denmark for centuries, joining the Swedish kingdom only in 1658. Many Danish influences remain, particularly in the architecture, language, and way of life.

The cities

Skåne's major cities lie along the western coast, facing Denmark and the waters of the Öresund. The ports of Helsingborg, Landskrona, and Malmö are linked by boat with Denmark. A hydrofoil service between Malmö and Copenhagen makes regular trips in only 35 minutes.

Helsingborg is a town with a continental flavor. Once the residence of Danish kings, and frequently a battle-ground, Helsingborg today is one of Sweden's larger cities. You'll want to visit the Kärnan, or Keep, all that remains of the one-time fortress; stroll down the walking streets of the shopping district; wander along Storgatan with its old buildings, St. Mary's Church, and museum; and visit the park-like open-air museum.

The 17th-century fortifications surrounding Landskrona Castle are some of Europe's best-preserved relics.

After Lund was founded by the Danish king Canute the Great, it was for four centuries the commercial, political, cultural, and religious capital of much of northern Europe. The founding of Lund University in the 1660s infused new intellectual stimulation. Lund's historic cathedral contains many of the city's treasures, the most famous being an astronomical clock (see it "perform" daily at noon). Tradesmen and shrewd shoppers bargain at the colorful market at Mårtenstorget. Visit Lund's fine outdoor cultural museum (see page 141) and the unusual Archive for Decorative Art.

Malmö, Skåne's commercial center, contains a large shipyard and industrial complex. You can explore the

Dag Hammarskjöld memorial is Backåkra, his farmhouse on the southern coast, where he planned to retire. *Furnishings include gifts he received while Secretary-General of the United Nations.*

Centuries-old buildings *in Lund's outdoor cultural museum range from patrician houses to wooden churches and sod-roofed barns (left). The province of Skåne is Sweden's vacationland and château country. Near Lund is Trolleholm Castle, one of the region's show-places (right).*

red brick fortress of Malmöhus Castle, cruise the harbor and canals in a sightseeing boat, and perhaps take in a performance at the top-flight Municipal Theater.

Along the sunny coast

In July and August, coastal resorts teem with visitors in search of sun, sea, and sights, but in June and September you'll be able to enjoy them in more leisurely fashion. Several of the towns – Ystad, Simrishamn, Kristianstad – have preserved a number of medieval half-timbered buildings. You can see Viking runestones and ancient stone monuments and grave fields.

South of Malmö on a small peninsula are the charming twin villages of Falsterbo and Skanör. Ystad is another popular resort with a fine curving stretch of wide sandy beach. More than 400 half-timbered buildings line the town's winding streets.

Most impressive of the ancient stone monuments is Ales Stenar near Kåseberga. Sweden's largest grave field, it dates from the early Viking Age. Its vertical stones form the outline of a ship, more than 70 yards long, pointing out to sea.

Dag Hammarskjöld purchased the old farmstead of Backåkra as a home for his retirement years, but the residence was not furnished until after his death. This property on the Kåseberga ridge overlooking the Baltic is now a memorial and nature reserve (open to visitors June through August).

Heading up the peninsula's eastern coast, you can visit the medieval stronghold of Glimmingehus and stop in Simrishamn, a pleasant village popular with artists. Kivik, in the center of orchards, has an ancient royal grave dating from 1400 B.C., a huge mound of boulders

and stones. Just off the main highway at Degeberga in thick beech forest is the Forsakar waterfall.

Although its population multiplies during the summer tourist invasion, Åhus has retained a charming small-town character. Inland is the city of Kristianstad, founded in 1614 as a fortified Danish merchant town. Only the moat and outer walls remain from the fortress. The city's most striking sight is the impressive Trefaldighets church, dating from the 17th century. Beyond the town, bird life flourishes in the reeds, bog-meadows, and shallow lakes formed by the Helgeån River.

Castles to visit

One of Skåne's greatest attractions is the large number of castles and manor houses scattered over the province. Most are still inhabited and can be visited only by special arrangement, but a few castles are open to the public in summer. Among the most renowned are these four:

Bäckaskog Castle, six miles east of Kristianstad just off route 15, is a 700-year-old château with hotel facilities, centered around a medieval cloister. It has gardens, woodland, and lakes.

Bosjökloster Castle, northwest of Hörby, is a former convent on Lake Ringsjön, with terraced gardens descending to the lake. Exhibits of handicrafts and contemporary art are featured.

Christinehof Castle lies a few miles northwest of Eljaröd near the Ystad-Kristianstad road. Built in the 1730s, the castle has never been altered nor modernized.

Svaneholm Castle, north of Skurup, was originally built for defense, later partially remodeled to resemble a Venetian palazzo.

Open-air folk museums

They recreate farm and village life of another era

In the Scandinavian countries, museum towns are a special pleasure. Open-air folk villages preserve the architecture and life of an earlier time. Many of the museum towns are rural in nature, but some recreate town life of a century or two ago.

Farm buildings, complete with animals, are a feature of some folk museums. Depending on the region, you may see thatched cottages or sod-roofed log cabins, timbered brick houses or plank-sided dwellings. Many of the buildings have been furnished in period style, including utensils and tools. Shops sometimes announce their business with interesting wooden or wrought iron signs — candles or a boot, a wooden cask or a baker's pretzel.

Often you can watch demonstrations of such old-time crafts as book-binding, glass-blowing, pottery-making, printing, spinning, and weaving. Some museums present programs of folk music and dances.

Most of the folk museums are open only in summer (usually from May to September), but check locally regarding dates and hours of any you plan to visit.

The folk museums listed below are just a sampling of those you'll find on your journey through Scandinavia.

In Norway

Old farm buildings have been preserved in several dozen regional museums throughout Norway.

The excellent *Norwegian Folk Museum* at Bygdöy, just west of Oslo, has a vast collection of more than 150 old wooden buildings collected from all over Norway and grouped in hamlets to represent different districts. Don't miss the 12th-century stave church, moved here from Gol. One section of the museum is a reconstructed 18th-century town.

Rural buildings are scattered over the grounds in a natural setting at *Maihaugen*, north of Oslo on the outskirts of Lillehammer. This collection emphasizes the folk culture of the Gudbrandsdalen, one of the most prosperous country districts in Norway. In the crafts museum you can see demonstrations by professional craftsmen.

The *Trondheim and Tröndelag Folk Museum* is located outside Trondheim at the medieval fortress of Sverresborg. More than sixty old buildings are grouped here. In addition to a large collection of farm buildings, one section is devoted to old Trondheim with merchants' houses, another to the Lapp culture.

Town life in past centuries is the theme of *Gamle Bergen*, located near the entrance to Bergen's harbor. Old buildings from the town have been moved here and arranged along cobblestone streets and alleys. Houses are furnished in early 19th-century style.

In Sweden

Old Sweden comes to life in Stockholm's *Skansen*, just a few minutes from the center of town. More than 100 buildings from all over the country have been collected

Furnished farmhouse at Skansen open-air museum in Stockholm is typical of Sweden's Dalecarlia region.

Shop signs lend a provocative accent to a cobbled Danish street in the Old Town museum in Århus (left). Helsinki's Seurasaari museum has many old rural Finnish buildings (top). Cows and chickens add to farm atmosphere at Lyngby, near Copenhagen (center). In summer Norwegian dancers entertain at a folk museum near Oslo (right).

here. In the town quarter, craftsmen demonstrate old-time crafts, and in summer there are folk dances and music. Look for a Lapp camp and reindeer enclosure in the 75-acre park.

Sod-roofed rural buildings and elegant manor houses have been gathered from throughout southern Sweden and reconstructed in Lund's *Kulturen.* Vying for your attention are rune stones and Viking implements, quaint stores and cottages, an old wooden church, and a farm complete with goats and geese.

The *Gammelgården* at Rättvik, on the shores of Lake Siljan in Dalarna province, is a complete old Dalecarlian farm, moved from different villages in the parish of Rättvik. You'll see ancient timbered houses with furniture and utensils, rustic wall paintings, and local costumes.

If you'll be in Sweden during the Midsummer festivities (the weekend nearest June 23-24), inquire about any special events. During Sweden's favorite holiday the maypoles go up outside farms and hotels, folk costumes are worn, and dancing goes on all night.

In Denmark

Best known of Denmark's open-air museums is the *Old Town* in Århus. More than fifty houses and shops have been assembled from all parts of the country and set up along cobblestone lanes. Buildings show the development of Danish urban life from about 1600 to 1850, with furnishings in period style, including utensils and tools. Plays and concerts are presented in the theater.

North of Copenhagen in the suburb of *Lyngby*, Dan-ish farm buildings, windmills, and country houses have been moved to a 40-acre rural park from all parts of Denmark and furnished with household effects representing the various Danish districts and periods.

Funen Village, south of Odense, includes a fine collection of buildings reconstructed to present a picture of village life a century or two ago (see page 144).

An Iron Age village has been reconstructed on a large heather-clad moor around Flynder Lake, at *Hjerl Hede* in northern Jutland south of Skive. Houses, farms, mills, churches, and schools are temporarily repopulated in summer so that visitors may see how people lived and worked in the Bronze and Iron Ages.

In Finland

The island of *Seurasaari* is the setting for Helsinki's open-air museum. Old Finnish peasant buildings have been assembled here from all over Finland. In an open-air theater, folk dancing is featured.

Turku's unusual *Handicrafts Museum* is located in a group of wooden houses, survivors of a disastrous 1827 fire that destroyed most of the town. In several dozen small shops you can see how craftsmen actually lived and worked in the nineteenth century. Among the crafts represented are violin maker, pipe maker, comb maker, and carriage builder. In summer you'll see demonstrations using techniques and tools of 150 years ago.

Porvoo, one of Finland's oldest towns, has preserved an old section near the cathedral that was planned according to the medieval town site.

Jutland's friendly villages

Prowl cobblestone lanes, look for storks, or jump into the North Sea

People who love the wide open spaces find Jutland's west coast a perfect side trip. Long sandy beaches backed by high grassy dunes edge the North Sea, where centuries ago Viking ships sailed forth on distant raiding and trading expeditions. Inland you'll find the thriving farms and friendly villages of rural Denmark. Here is the country's oldest town with its nesting storks. You can make side excursions to two offshore islands before you head back to more-traveled tourist routes.

The larger towns have modern hotel accommodations, but you may decide to spend the night in a simple *kro*, one of numerous rustic country inns which dot the countryside. Many of these cheery roadside guesthouses are hundreds of years old, and some of them have been run by the same hospitable family for many generations.

You'll find local tourist associations happy to help if you would like to spend a week with a farm family or rent a summer cottage. They can also tell you where you can rent bicycles for the day, or where to find the local fish auction or the open-air market.

The Jutland peninsula is the only part of Scandinavia connected to the mainland. Because this westernmost part of Denmark is bordered on the south by Germany, contrasting political and cultural ties have pulled at the region for centuries. Denmark's southernmost province of Schleswig was under German rule from 1864 until after World War I.

Marshland villages

Several enticing villages lie along the German border in Denmark's southwestern corner, in fertile marsh-meadows only a few feet above sea level. Once periodic floods caused tremendous damage and loss of life here, but now the region is protected from the sea by great embankments.

Largest of the towns is Tönder, known for both its lacemaking industry and its attractive houses. If you stroll down Uldgate, Östergade, or Vestergade, you can see the characteristic gabled roofs, projecting bay windows, and artful doorways.

Three miles to the west is the drowsy village of Mögeltönder, whose main street some people think is the most beautiful in Denmark. Thatched, bay-windowed houses and sweet-smelling lime trees line the street. You'll find the village church and an 18th-century baroque manor house nearby in a large park.

The center of Rudböl's main street marks the Danish-German border. The dividing line is marked only by a few metal discs set into the brick-paved street.

Ribe is Denmark's oldest city. You can climb the cathedral tower for a view over the city's red rooftops.

Swimming beaches on island of Fanö
(top) are popular with Danish families.
Lime trees and thatched houses line the
main street of Mögeltönder (bottom).
Children find the narrow streets of
Tönder perfect for cycling (right).

The windswept coast

Jutland's long, clean, west coast beaches are Denmark's vacationland. As soon as the cold weather is over, when the fields turn green and the sun is high in the sky, Danes get the seasonal urge to jump into the water for a swim. Everyone, regardless of age or shape, plunges in from June until September. Bathing is the country's national sport, the Danes and their guests making maximum use of the beaches and the sea.

In May and September you may well have this spectacular coast almost to yourself. Before and after the Danish school holidays, few people will be around. You can stride alone over the smooth white sands in the invigorating air or soak up the warm sun from a sheltered hollow in the dunes.

Island side trips

Two offshore islands along this southern coast are favorite resorts. West of Skærbæk is the island of Römö, connected to the mainland by a six-mile causeway. Along its western shore is Denmark's widest beach. An 18th-century farm has been restored as a museum, the Kommandörgården, illustrating some of the island's whaling traditions. You can also visit the fishing harbor in Havneby.

To the north is the island of Fanö, accessible by a 20-minute ferry ride from Esbjerg. In summer the weathered buildings are alive with activity as, like generations of Danish families, modern Danes enjoy the splendid 10-mile-long beach. In the fishing village of Sönderho, at the island's southern tip, you recall Fanö's seafaring past as you visit the small church hung with model ships and walk along the town's narrow streets past old skippers' cottages.

Denmark's oldest city

Inland a few miles from the coast is Ribe, Denmark's oldest city. Founded in the 9th century, Ribe was already an important settlement when its cathedral was built about 1100. One of Scandinavia's most well-known churches, its tower dominates the town. If you're feeling energetic, climb to the viewing platform for a far-ranging view over the city and surrounding marshland.

In the Middle Ages Ribe was Denmark's most important western port. Merchants returned here from their long voyages with exotic merchandise. More than a hundred medieval buildings have been preserved in the town. You'll find many of them on crooked streets and cozy lanes off the main thoroughfares. Cobblestone walkways still guide foot traffic among the half-timbered houses and small gardens. The outstanding Black Friars Abbey, dating from the 13th century, is one of Europe's best-preserved and most beautiful monasteries. If you're in Ribe on a summer evening, observe the night watchman making his traditional rounds.

Esbjerg is modern Denmark's main western gateway. The city has the only deep water port on Jutland's west coast, with regular passenger service between Esbjerg and Britain. It's a busy export harbor for Denmark's agricultural products, the home of a large fishing fleet. If you're an early riser, take a pre-breakfast walk to the lively fish auction for the action beginning at 7 A.M.

Modern Danish art is displayed at the Kunstpavillon. And don't miss Esbjerg's fascinating Fishery and Maritime Museum.

Island-hopping in Denmark

Summer is the time to visit the delightful central islands

Funen, Denmark's garden island, radiates a tranquillity that is a comforting contrast to this bustling jet age. The countryside of Hans Christian Andersen is at its prettiest in summer, when the wheat is standing yellow, the oats green, and hay is stacked in the grassy meadows. Red Danish cattle graze in the rich pastures and plod peacefully home in the evening. Hollyhocks grow tall, splashing color throughout neat cottage gardens.

Driving is pleasant on Funen's uncrowded roads and winding byways, and island-hopping in the archipelago south of Funen adds an enjoyable extra dimension. You can easily reach the three large islands—Tåsinge, Langeland, and Aerö—by bridge or ferry. Each has numerous diversions for you to explore.

Bicycling is the main mode of transportation on Funen, as elsewhere in Denmark; practically everyone rides a bicycle—except the foreign tourist. If you'd like to join the cycling Danes for a day on wheels, you can rent a bicycle in Odense or in other large towns. Your hotel or the local tourist office can suggest routes and direct you to the nearest bicycle rental shop.

Denmark's low, gently undulating land is ideal for bicycle touring; the everchanging wayside scene lends continual interest. You'll pedal along coastline roads, through wooded regions, and past old villages where friendly Danes greet you with a cheery wave. Separate cycling paths often parallel the roads. The marine climate never gets extremely hot, and there's always a breeze. April, May, and June are the months of least rainfall; later in summer you may have to dodge showers more often.

The town of Hans Christian Andersen

Funen's largest city, Odense, is best known as the birthplace of Hans Christian Andersen. A statue of Denmark's great writer of fairy tales stands in the city park. You can visit two houses associated with his childhood.

According to tradition, Hans was born in a house at Hans Jensensstræde 39-43, the son of a poor cobbler and an alcoholic mother. The house is now a museum, where you'll see mementoes of his life and writings, including his writing desk, his top hat, and his famous umbrella.

Andersen spent his childhood in the humble house at Munkemöllestræde 3, now also a museum. Here in one small room the family lived and slept, and Father Andersen plied his cobbling trade.

South of the city is Funen Village (*Den Fynske Landsby*), a delightful collection of thatched farmhouses, half-timbered cottages, mills, and other buildings reconstructed among the woods as a typical village in Funen in the 18th and 19th centuries. The village is open daily from April through October. Take a bus (line 2) from the town of Odense. In midsummer the fairy tales of Hans Christian Andersen are dramatized in the village's outdoor theater.

From May to mid-September you can take a boat ride on the tree-lined Odense River. For information on de-

Troense, on the island of Tåsinge, is now connected by bridge to Funen. Don't miss the town's fishing port.

Island of Funen *provides plenty of activities for visitors. You can stroll through Fåborg's Gamlegård district of old-style buildings (top left), see farm buildings and animals in the Funen Village near Odense (bottom left), rent a bicycle for a day—here in Fåborg (center bottom), or visit the gardens of Egeskov Castle (right).*

parture times, check with the Odense Tourist Office in the town hall or at your local hotel.

South to Svendborg

One of Denmark's most attractive castles lies just off the main road south of Ringe. Mirrored in its encircling moat, towered and turreted Egeskov Castle has all the characteristics of a proper fairy-tale palace, including a drawbridge and thirty acres of formal gardens. The castle was built about 1550, during a period of civil wars, as a private fortress. Huge pilings rammed deep into the earth formed the foundations; the rose-colored brick walls appear to rise directly from the water. The castle is not open to visitors, but you can stroll in the park.

Svendborg is an old sailing town that successfully combines the traditional with the modern look. You can learn something of the town's maritime history in the local museum (Fruestræde 3).

Island hopping

From Svendborg you can make boat and ferry trips to a number of islands in the South Funen archipelago; our route takes in the three largest—Tåsinge, Langeland, and Aerö. You can reach the first two by bridges, but you'll need to take a ferry to Aerö.

Idyllic Tåsinge is an island of billowing grain fields and thick beech groves, with an occasional village breaking the horizon. Many buildings are capped with thatched roofs in Troense, the main town. Here you can visit the castle of Valdemar Slot, dating from 1640 and serving now as a naval museum. At Bregninge, stop at the windmill for a superb view.

Langeland is the largest of the three islands. Its main town of Rudköbing has charming old streets. The road north passes Tranekær Castle, built as a royal fortress about 1200.

From Rudköbing it is a one hour ferry ride to Aerö, the most captivating of the islands. The old seafaring town of Marstal—home port of many of Denmark's ships—has the tang of tar and seawater. Delightful Aerösköbing is the place for an overnight stop. Its lamp posts, cobblestone streets, and quaint old houses take you back to another century. Bus service connects Aerösköbing with Marstal and the fishing village of Söby.

Car ferries also operate between Aerösköbing and Svendborg and between Söby and Fåborg. On weekends and during vacation periods, reserve ferry space to avoid delay (see page 151).

Fåborg is surrounded by wooded, rolling lands and overlooks its own fjord. Now only one of the town gates remains of the original walled city. A museum in the tall belfry contains an outstanding collection of paintings by modern Danish artists.

West of Fåborg is the unusual Horne Round Church, the only one of its type on the island. Once both church and fortress, with walls seven feet thick, today only the core of the building remains. A mile north of Horne, a 500-year-old water mill has been turned into a museum.

Cruising inland waterways

Trips by paddle steamer, canal boat, hydrofoil, riverboat

In Scandinavia one is never far from the water. All four of the northern countries are bordered in part by the sea. Trips by boat—to the fjord country, to offshore islands, to North Cape—have long been a favorite activity for visitors to Scandinavia.

You can make equally enjoyable boat trips on the inland waterways of Denmark, Norway, Sweden, and Finland. Lake, river, and canal trips show off the epic northern scenery in a leisurely manner.

Below are a sampling of passenger trips available, varying in length from a half day to a week. More information on a particular trip may be obtained from the tourist office of the country (addresses on page 151).

On Denmark's Silkeborg lakes

Silkeborg's lake district in central Jutland includes some of Denmark's most stunning scenery. The town lies on the banks of the Gudenå River, which winds through a chain of shallow lakes surrounded by wooded hills. From mid-May to mid-September, the paddlewheel-steamer *Hjejlen*, built in 1861, and smaller boats make daily trips on the lakes southeast from Silkeborg to Himmelbjerget and Ry.

Through rugged Norway

In Norway's rugged countryside, where rail and road building is tremendously expensive, lakes, rivers, and fjords have been natural traffic arteries since Viking days.

The longest waterway still used in southern Norway is the Telemark Canal, running from the fjord at Skien, on the southern coast, to Dalen in the heart of Telemark. From early June through mid-August, the canal boat *Victoria* leaves Skien three mornings a week on its all-day trip, returning from Dalen on alternate days. The memorable 65-mile water route goes through locks on the Skien and Bandak canals, along rivers and broad woodland lakes, and past mountains where farmsteads perch and waterfalls cascade.

North of Oslo, the century-old paddle-steamer *Skibladner* cruises Lake Mjösa daily from mid-June to mid-

August, passing fertile farmland, lakeside settlements, and forested hills. The boat makes one round trip daily between Eidsvoll and Lillehammer, with brief stops at Hamar and Gjövik; the boat leaves Eidsvoll in mid-morning on its 5½-hour trip to the head of the lake, then returns from Lillehammer in the afternoon. Connecting train service runs between Oslo and Eidsvoll.

In the remote northland of Finnmark, transportation is by narrow, flat-bottomed Lapp riverboat. On the Tana River (the boundary between Norway and Finland), motor-powered riverboats provide passenger service twice a week during July and August. Passengers surrounded by mail, luggage, and other travelers sit in rather cramped positions on the floor, while a helmsman guides the boat through silent frontier country sprinkled with Lapp villages and farms.

A two-day trip goes from Karasjok to Skipagurra, with overnight accommodations ashore at Levajok. The Finnish mail boat also takes passengers on its tri-weekly runs (from Karigasniemi via Levajok to Utsjoki), or you can go along on the daily milk-boat run from Karasjok. Fishermen may decide to stay longer when they learn that 60-lb. salmon are caught every season in the Tana.

Sweden's canals and lakes

Canals connecting Sweden's lakes and rivers were originally built to move freight within and across the country. But today most of the activity comes from pleasure traffic. A leisurely cruise by canal boat offers a relaxing way to see some of the Swedish countryside.

One of the best-known boat trips in Europe is the three-day cruise along the Gota Canal, crossing central Sweden from Gothenburg on the west to Stockholm on the east. The canal connects Lake Vänern and Lake Vättern, then continues eastward to the Baltic Sea. Sailings are scheduled from mid-May to early September. On the 347-mile route you sail across wide lakes, pass through 65 locks, and cruise through narrow, grass-edged channels where overhanging trees occasionally brush your boat as it glides beneath.

The Kinda Canal provides an opportunity to see the

Travel by boat can include cruises on lakes, rivers, and canals. A cruise boat glides along the Kinda Canal (*top left*); a century-old paddlesteamer plies the Silkeborg lakes (*bottom left*). Going through locks is part of the fun on the Telemark Canal (*right*).

verdant forests and magnificent castles of Östergötland province, one of Sweden's most scenic regions. Day trips on the canal leave Linköping from mid-May through August. The canal begins at Lake Roxen and follows lakes and rivers south for about 55 miles, passing through 15 locks on the seven-hour trip to Rimforsa Bridge.

Dalarna province is the heart of Sweden; the Lake Siljan region is the center of Dalarna. Located northwest of Stockholm, you can reach the district in a three-hour train ride from the capital. Summer cruises on Lake Siljan leave daily from Rättvik. On a short trip you'll see attractive villages along the shore, each with its "maypole" that remains decorated the year around. If you can, plan to be here for Midsummer Eve celebrations, when costumed villagers arrive in long, narrow "church-boats" for the all-night dancing and festivities.

Finnish lake trips

Innumerable lakes (estimates go as high as 60,000) spangle Finland's terrain, rivers lace its interior, and forests cover most of the remaining countryside. Varied and frequent lake trips penetrate this wilderness.

Boats operate from June through August. All of them have a restaurant aboard; those offering extended trips provide cabins. Connecting transportation by train and bus permits you to make circular tours on one inclusive excursion ticket.

From Hämeenlinna, the Finnish Silver Line heads north to Tampere through a lavish chain of lakes and narrow channels. The ship arrives in time for you to return to Helsinki the same day if you wish. Or you may decide to stay overnight in Finland's second largest city and continue northward on the route known as the Poet's Way—up Lake Näsijärvi to Virrat.

The only hydrofoil operating on Finnish lakes plies Lake Päijänne between Lahti and Jyväskylä during the summer months. The *Tehi* makes the 75-mile trip in about three hours. For those who prefer more leisurely boat travel, the steamboat *Suomi* makes the Jyväskylä-Lahti trip on Mondays in summer, returning on Wednesdays to Jyväskylä. The *Suomi* also makes evening cruises and a Sunday picnic cruise from Jyväskylä.

In the alluring Saimaa Lake district of eastern Finland, you can relax on a seven-day, 600-mile cruise over the island-dotted lakes, or you can take numerous shorter trips in the region. Savonlinna is the center of the district. From it, daily summer service connects with the main towns of Kuopio, Joensuu, Lappeenranta, and Mikkeli.

Turku, Finland's oldest city

This historic town makes a fine base for excursions

Easily accessible from both Stockholm and Helsinki, Finland's oldest and third largest city, Turku, gives you a feeling of both the country's past and present. The city also makes a good base for trips up and down the coast and to the islands of the Turku archipelago.

You can drive to Turku from Helsinki (about 100 miles) or take one of the frequent trains speeding between the two cities. From Stockholm, there is daily ferry and plane service to Turku by way of Mariehamn in the Åland Islands.

From the 13th century until the early 1800s, Turku was Finland's most important city. The capital of the country was moved to Helsinki in 1812, however, and a disastrous fire leveled most of Turku's wooden buildings fifteen years later.

Commercially, the city is Finland's gate to the West; in fact, the word *turku* means trading post. The busy all-year port is especially important in winter when northern ports are inaccessible. Turku is the site of Finland's largest shipyards and its leading tobacco factory.

A walk through the city

For many centuries the Aura River was Turku's traffic artery. A walk along the river bank reveals the heart of the town: old Turku around the Cathedral, the Town Hall (don't miss the busy and colorful outdoor market), the modern Municipal Theater, shipyards, and finally at the river's mouth, the ancient fortress of Turku Castle.

The 700-year-old Turku Cathedral is a city landmark, its tower rising above the trees. Built, enlarged, and altered over the centuries, the church shows a variety of architectural influences. After having been gutted by fire in 1827, it was completely restored.

One of the few areas to be spared in the disastrous 1827 fire was Luostarinmäki (Cloister Hill), now known for its unique Handicrafts Museum (see page 141). In the years following the fire, craftsmen congregated here to live and work. Various crafts are demonstrated in summer.

The buildings of 19th-century Turku are gradually being replaced by buildings of very modern design. The distinctive municipal theater alongside the river is one example, the striking concert hall another. You can visit the Sibelius Museum, devoted to Finland's famous composer, view paintings and sculptures by Wäinö Aaltonen, and see collections of old and modern Finnish art.

Visiting Turku Castle

The historic fortress of Turku Castle, standing on a rocky island at the mouth of the Aura River, dates back to about 1280 (when Finland was part of the Swedish kingdom).

Besieged at least six times during Scandinavian wars during the 16th century, the castle has been the home of rulers. Many royal guests have stayed within its thick walls. Twice gutted by fire, the castle was allowed to deteriorate for several hundred years. Following a 15-year restoration project, completed in 1961, the castle is once again a showplace open to visitors. The Turku Historical Museum is located in part of the castle; religious services are held regularly in the castle church.

Tree-lined promenade along the Aura River is pleasant for strolling. Many residents moor pleasure boats here.

Handicrafts Museum *is housed in a group of old buildings that survived the 1827 fire (left). Turku Cathedral (center), a city landmark, is over 700 years old. In summer frequent trips leave the city for the rocky islands of the Turku archipelago (top). The beach resort of Naantali (right) is the summer home of Finland's President.*

Excursions outside the city

Outside Turku, one of the favorite excursions is to the nearby beach resort of Naantali, summer residence of the President of Finland. The town grew up around a convent; now its renovated chapel serves as the local church. Nearby is the charming old part of town with narrow streets and wooden houses.

If you want to spend a day in the country, seek out some of the medieval grey stone churches and old manors in the patterned farmland around Turku. Just outside of town, visit the modern Resurrection Chapel in Turku Cemetery.

Ruissalo National Park, on an island 20 minutes from Turku by boat, is the site of Finland's largest campground, offering a sandy beach and a sturdy oak forest.

Trips to nearby islands

Island fanciers will be drawn to Finland's unspoiled southern coast, speckled with rocky isles. As you cruise through the Turku archipelago in summer, you'll often see sunbathers or swimmers. If total privacy appeals to you, rent your own island and cottage (see page 151).

Water buses leave from Aura Bridge in Turku on frequent trips to many of the islands in the archipelago.

The more distant Åland Islands are a popular holiday destination during the brief Finnish summer. On the Swedish-speaking island group, a seafaring tradition survives. Tangible reminders of a vigorous maritime history fill the museum in Mariehamn.

EATING ADVENTURES

A healthy appetite and a willingness to try new foods can go far in providing new experiences and pleasant memories. The curious traveler who is not afraid to try an unfamiliar dish often makes a delicious discovery. Even the not-too-adventuresome eater—with a bit of advance homework—can enjoy his favorite foods prepared in the European manner.

Before you go, familiarize yourself with the foreign words (depending on the countries you plan to visit), so you can distinguish beef from poultry, pork from fish. Look up the names of several of your favorite vegetables and fruits. Many guidebooks list the terms, and you'll find many words similar to their English equivalents.

In your reading, make notes of regional food specialties that you'd like to try. Some government tourist offices provide information on traditional dishes. Basic guidebooks often have a chapter describing the national or regional cuisine. Foreign cookbooks are a good source of ideas.

Adventurous sampling need not be confined to conventional restaurants. Have lunch at a *broodje* sandwich bar in Amsterdam, followed by Dutch cookies from a local bakery. Seek out a *crèperie* in Paris. Sample the traditional *weisswurst* at Munich's lively open-air market. Enjoy a Belgian waffle at a traveling fair. Order *pissaladière* in a Riviera cafe. When you're buying picnic supplies, select an interesting-looking *paté*, an unfamiliar cheese, or a small *quiche*.

Meeting the Scandinavians

Here are programs to help you get acquainted

Scandinavian hospitality goes far beyond the smile of a hotel concierge; it penetrates into the workshops, factories, schools, and homes of the people.

Denmark, Norway, and Sweden all have hospitality programs encouraging visitors to make personal contacts with local individuals and families having similar business, cultural, or hobby interests. Participating Scandinavian hosts can always speak the language of their guests.

You can gather information about each country's program from the appropriate tourist office (addresses on page 151), but final arrangements are confirmed by the local tourist organization only after you actually arrive in a city. Usually 48 hours notice is necessary. No accommodation is involved, nor is there any cost.

Many Scandinavian families are away from home on their own vacations during the months of July and August, so you'll have your best opportunity for contacts in other months.

Meet the Danes. Visits are arranged by personal application to the local tourist offices in the following cities: Århus, Aalborg, Esbjerg, Fredericia, Herning, Horsens, Kolding, Nyborg, Odense, Silkeborg, Skanderborg, and Skive.

Know the Norwegians. Write in advance if possible, or apply in person, to the Oslo Travel Association (Raadhusgaten 19) giving details on your interests and expected date of arrival.

Similar programs for visitors are operated in Bergen and Stavanger.

Sweden at Home. Before you leave, fill in a form—available from the Swedish National Tourist Office—listing your profession, hobbies, and date of arrival. Arrangements may be made through the local or regional tourist organization in the following towns: Gothenburg, Eskilstuna, Falkenberg, Falun, Helsingborg, Kalmar, Karlshamn, and Karlstad.

Other towns participating in the program are Linköping, Lund, Malmö, Nyköping, Örebro, Östersund, Ronneby, Skellefteå, Umeå, Varberg, Visby, and Växjö.

Scandinavia at work

Many industries are pleased to receive visitors from abroad and show them around. Local and regional tourist offices can tell you which companies have visitor facilities and often will help you make arrangements when advance notice is necessary.

During summer months, "lifeseeing" tours are available in Copenhagen and Stockholm, giving visitors a close-up view of the latest trends in Scandinavian social welfare and arts, crafts, and design.

Group workshops can be arranged in a number of professional fields—environmental protection; architecture and city planning; arts, crafts, and design; social welfare; medicine; furniture manufacturing; agriculture; and forestry. For information on workshop programs, write to Manager, Special Interest Travel, Scandinavian Airlines, 138-02 Queens Boulevard, Jamaica, N. Y. 11435.

Friendly Danish schoolchildren get acquainted with visitors. Scandinavian children learn English in school.

IN SCANDINAVIA: special interests

SCANDINAVIAN DESIGN • Shopping in Scandinavia is a feast for the eyes. Designers combine function with beauty and bold design, and you'll see many tastefully-designed objects for the home – ceramics and china, glass and crystal, rugs and textiles, silver and stainless and pewter, furniture, and handicrafts of all kinds.

Each capital city has a permanent design exhibition with a selection of the best in the country's arts and crafts. You'll find this an excellent place to begin your shopping search, particularly if time is limited.

In Stockholm the permanent exhibition is Form Design Center, Sveavägen 17; in Copenhagen you should visit Den Permanente, on Vesterport, near the central rail station; in Helsinki the permanent exhibition of crafts is the Finnish Design Center, Kasarmikatu 19; in Oslo stop at the Forum, Rosenkrantzgate 7, the permanent sales exhibit, or Norwegian Designs, Stortingsgate 28.

SWEDISH GLASS WORKS • You can watch glassblowers at work in many of the Swedish glass works. Over 80 per cent of the manufacturers are concentrated in the southeastern part of the country, between Kalmar and Växjö. For information on companies that welcome visitors, write to the Swedish National Tourist Office.

FARMHOUSE HOLIDAYS • Farm families throughout Denmark are now opening their doors to visitors who wish to spend a week or more enjoying the pleasant, simple life in the Danish countryside. For more information, write to the Danish Tourist Office. Accommodations are arranged through local tourist associations.

Finnish farmers also will rent guest rooms (with some meals included) for visitors who would like to live with a friendly farm family. For more information, write to the Finland National Tourist Office.

TAPIOLA GARDEN CITY • Town planning at its best can be seen in the thriving community of Tapiola, six miles west of Helsinki. Experts in architecture, sociology, civil engineering, landscape gardening, domestic science, and child and youth welfare have teamed to plan a modern, self-contained town of 16,000. Green areas, trees, and gardens form an important part of the environment. Buses leave frequently from the Helsinki Bus Station to Tapiola.

HOBBY VACATIONS • Combine a relaxing vacation in Scandinavia with your own interests or hobbies.

In Norway you can participate in mountaineering courses, horse riding and pony trekking vacations, sailing and yachting schools, fishing trips, and work camps. Sweden has physical fitness programs, fishing and hunting trips, riding camps, walking and hiking tours. In Denmark you can go on fishing or sailing excursions, cycling trips, or attend riding schools. Finland offers gold-panning excursions, hiking, and fishing trips. Additional information on any of the programs is available from the appropriate tourist office.

CAR FERRY SPACE • Motorists traveling by ferry within Denmark (or between Denmark and surrounding countries) should request the *Car Ferries* folder from the Danish National Tourist Office. To avoid delays, advance reservations are recommended on the busier routes, particularly during the main travel months.

HIKING AND WALKING TRIPS • Visitors who wish to sample the outdoor life will find a fine network of trails available. The hiking season extends from late June to early September.

The Swedish Touring Club maintains more than 1400 miles of marked trails, dotted with a number of mountain huts and mountain stations. The organization publishes a booklet, *Hiking in the Swedish Highlands*, available from the Swedish Touring Club, FACK, 103 80 Stockholm, Sweden.

In Norway's principal mountain areas, tourist lodges where meals and overnight accommodations are available are operated by the Norwegian Touring Club. Walking tours are conducted each summer; for detailed information, write to the Norwegian Touring Club, Stortingsgate 28, Oslo 1.

In Finland seek out opportunities for forest and lakeside walks and for hiking in the sub-Arctic terrain of Lapland. For a booklet on hiking routes in Finnish Lapland, write the Finland National Tourist Office.

NORWAY'S STAVE CHURCHES • Ranking high among the famous attractions of Norway are the richly carved wooden stave churches, with their dragons' heads and serpent ornaments, scattered over the countryside. Only 32 of the churches remain of the original 750 built during the Middle Ages. Information on the churches and a suggested tour can be obtained from the Norwegian National Tourist Office.

SUMMER COTTAGES • Cabins, chalets, and cottages ringed with beautiful scenery can be rented by the week in all four countries. Dwellings are usually equipped for vacation use, the renter needing to bring only linens and cutlery. The variety of private dwellings ranges from modern to primitive. You can rent your own log cabin in Norway or Sweden or your own Finnish island complete with cottage, sauna, and rowboat. For more information, write to the appropriate tourist office.

Scandinavian National Tourist Office
3600 Wilshire Boulevard, Los Angeles, Calif. 90010

Norwegian National Tourist Office
75 Rockefeller Plaza, New York, N.Y. 10019

Swedish National Tourist Office
75 Rockefeller Plaza, New York, N.Y. 10019

Danish National Tourist Office
75 Rockefeller Plaza, New York, N.Y. 10019

Finland National Tourist Office
75 Rockefeller Plaza, New York, N.Y. 10019

Traveling in Eastern Europe

For new experiences, visit the socialist lands

The map shows Eastern Europe with labels: BALTIC SEA, Leningrad, Moscow, U.S.S.R., EAST GERMANY, Berlin, POLAND, Warsaw, Prague, CZECHOSLOVAKIA, Kiev, HUNGARY, Budapest, Odessa, ROMANIA, Belgrade, Bucharest, YUGOSLAVIA, BULGARIA, BLACK SEA, Sofia, ADRIATIC SEA, Tirane, ALBANIA.

A vacation in Eastern Europe is no longer a voyage into the unknown, recommended only for the most daring travelers. Communist governments have discovered in recent years that coveted tourist dollars must be attracted by capitalistic means.

Accordingly, western visitors are pleasantly surprised to find they may buy souvenirs with American Express cards, sleep in an Intercontinental Hotel, or slip off into the countryside in a Hertz rental car—all behind the once forbidding Iron Curtain.

A visit to one or more of the socialist lands, as they like to call themselves, can more than repay the effort of preparation. Like Western Europe, the East also has its great art galleries, golden beaches, imposing churches, mountain drives, ancient castles, and colorful folklore. And whatever else may be said about the "planned economy," it generally means lower prices.

Despite improvements, however, the East Europeans have not been able to keep up in every respect with their tourist boom. That means, for example, that first class hotel rooms are often in short supply. A trip requires time for thorough advance planning—preferably with the aid of an experienced travel agent who has good European connections.

Getting started

Several sources can supply you with useful information about East European countries. A knowledgeable travel agent is one of your best bets. Your local public library may have books about some of the countries. Most of the East European governments maintain tourist information offices in New York City (addresses on page 157). Although they can't book tours for you, they will send a flood of colorful brochures in English. One U.S. airline (Pan American), the Soviet Aeroflot, and Czechoslovakia's CSA all have direct flights linking New York and Eastern Europe; their offices provide information.

Whether you want to go easy on your first trip or extend your West European vacation to a full continental spree, remember that it's often painless and inexpensive to add an eastern leg. Even a day or weekend trip from Vienna or Helsinki can enrich your itinerary. Tourist agencies in those capitals have neat little packages which can usually be arranged fairly simply and cheaply.

If you want something more extensive, such as a swing through several countries, by yourself or with a group, then you must start planning at home.

When to go

The East Europeans, like their West European neighbors, gear up for tourists (and take their own vacations) mainly from June through September. Don't forget there are weather extremes in the East, too, ranging from near-Arctic frosts to the Black Sea's balmy breezes. Some resort regions, notably along the Black Sea and Yugoslav coasts, have as many as four seasons, with matching seasonal price differences at hotels.

You can camp *in Eastern Europe, too—here in Russia. Tourist offices can provide camping information and maps.*

Gypsy musicians serenade diners in a rustic Romanian restaurant (left). Moscow river cruise (center) provides fine views of the Kremlin, palace at left in picture, and the city skyline. Costumed dancers wait their turn at a folk festival in northern Poland (right).

If you're one of the clever travelers who visits Europe in the spring or fall to avoid wrestling with crowds or peak prices, there's another point to check before heading east. The communist governments delight in organizing mammoth trade fairs and conferences in May and September or October. That means hotel shortages in secondary cities like Brno and Poznan and also in Budapest, Leipzig, and sometimes Moscow.

Visas — the necessary evil

"It's embarrassing to admit it," says an American diplomat with long experience in Eastern Europe, "but some of our countrymen still think all they have to do to cross any border is hold up that U.S. passport." Disillusionment often begins when the tourist drops into an airline office, wanting to fly to Moscow the next day.

It's true that Yugoslavia, Romania, and Bulgaria (which have been pushing their tourist programs hardest) have scrapped all but the formalities for most travelers and now issue visas at the frontier or on arrival at the airport. But it's still advisable to have that precious stamp in your passport before you arrive. Tourists with advance visas are processed first, of course. And crowded border crossings or delayed flights can lead to unpleasant scenes.

You can obtain a visa personally by applying at any consulate of the country concerned or by having an airline or travel agent do it for you. Passport size photos, a completed application form, and sometimes a fee of as much as $6 or $7 are usually required. Some countries will issue a visa on the spot; others take as long as three weeks. This is reason enough for planning your trip early. The travel agent will need your passport well in advance if you want to visit several countries.

East Germany and the Soviet Union are special cases. No visa will be issued until you have proof of reserved hotel rooms in the cities you want to visit. That means

a travel agent has to get confirmation from the Soviet Intourist or East German Travel Bureau before he can obtain your visa. But at least you'll never be turned away in these countries with a "Sorry, no vacancy."

Hotels, grand style and otherwise

With a little bit of luck, you may get into some of Europe's great old hotels at prices that are surprisingly reasonable. Still, too many people have heard of the delights of a stay in Budapest's Gellert Hotel or the Francuski in Cracow to make them really readily available. You can try reserving specific hotels through your travel agent, but the supply is often not up to the demand, and you're more likely to end up in one of the comfortable but plain government-built establishments.

Requesting a Moscow hotel by name usually costs an extra $10, and there's unfortunately no guarantee that you'll get your choice, unless you have the voucher with the hotel name. (Yes, it's still a good idea to take along a flat "all-size" sink stopper. There are still a few hotel bathrooms without them.)

Eating — nobody's spectator sport

Many veteran travelers swear that Hungarian cooking is Europe's best. Meat and fish soups in the Soviet Union are delightful. Ice cream gets better as you go east. The secret of good eating in Eastern Europe, as everywhere, lies in finding the specialties. Some advance homework with a good guidebook — or even a specialized cookbook — will help. Tour escorts usually can offer good suggestions. If you're traveling independently, ask one of the people in the official travel office; they're usually pleased to recommend both a restaurant and a specialty or two.

Menus in the major cities are almost always multilingual, but you may have to request one because they're

Travelers pause for a roadside picnic along a Romanian backroad (left). You buy picnic supplies in local shops and open-air markets; if words fail, you can always resort to sign language (bottom center). Late spring is harvest time in Bulgaria's Valley of the Roses (top). Yugoslavia's Plitvice lakes and waterfalls draw visitors inland (right).

sometimes in short supply. In any case, it never hurts to have a small pocket dictionary or phrase book handy.

Restaurant service ranges from impeccable in parts of Hungary and Yugoslavia to dreadful in Moscow. The Russians themselves lament their lackluster service, but as one comment goes: "When Russians get jobs as waiters, they become civil servants." The only recourse is to wait, often as long as two hours. If you're planning to dine in a good restaurant, you must reserve.

Avoiding the currency headache

Changing money and taking pictures are the two touchy points of travel in Eastern Europe. But you don't have a thing to fear if you remember that there are rules and they must be obeyed.

It's true that the official rate at which you must change your dollars in the East is paltry compared with the lure of the black market. And for every two people you tell about your planned trip, you will find one with a "foolproof" plan for getting cheap rubles into Russia or zlotys into Poland. But take it from the Old Hands: following anything other than the letter of the communist law in these countries is just plain foolhardy.

Travelers' checks, dollars, or almost any western currency remaining from your earlier wanderings may be exchanged for local money at practically all travel offices, banks, border crossing points, or airports.

Some countries require you to exchange a certain amount on entry—between $3 and $8 per day—to "cover" each day of your permitted visa stay, unless you are traveling pre-paid and have hotel vouchers in hand. Most tourists need at least this much for meals, hotels, and souvenirs. Anything above that which you haven't spent may be changed back to dollars on departure.

One very important rule: don't discard any piece of paper that you receive when changing money, and take special care of forms which have official-looking, rubber-stamped language. They can be vital in re-exchanging money and even in getting out of the country.

As mentioned earlier, credit cards have found their way to Eastern Europe. So far their use is limited to such major tourist center establishments as major hotels, restaurants, some car rentals, and souvenir shops. Using your credit card to cash private checks is still a thing of the future, however.

One way out of the currency exchange headache is the pre-paid trip, all details being arranged in advance at home or in a western capital and vouched for by coupons which you hand over to pay your hotel bill. That's how the Russians and East Germans require it, and you may find it convenient in other countries, as well. You'll know that everything has been done legally and at the official rate of exchange. But you will still probably want to change a few dollars for impulse purchases.

Be sure you know exactly how much is covered by your prepaid tour, though, and just what might be extra. For example, some travel agents won't bother with reserving opera or theater tickets.

Tipping? There too?

The classless society of Eastern Europe hasn't eliminated all bourgeois habits. You may occasionally meet a Russian, especially an Intourist guide, who is insulted at the attempted tip. But taxi drivers and porters can be quite insistent, if no authorities are looking. Outside the Soviet Union, a little something extra is expected by waiters, hotel porters and taxi drivers, just as in the West.

An American diplomat who regularly makes the rounds in the East solves the problem diplomatically by carrying a supply of Kennedy half dollars.

Getting there — and getting around

Most East European capitals can be reached from the U.S. with no more than one change of plane. Airport facilities have been vastly improved in the last few years, and the East European airlines have modern jet equipment, usually Russian made. Flights across national borders on these airlines are generally quite comfortable. Domestically, air travel is cheap; old but serviceable prop transports are used like buses. Although foreigners are welcome, reservations on internal flights are more difficult to get than on foreign stretches.

East Europeans use water transportation more than do westerners. Hydrofoils and passenger cruise ships that travel the Danube from the German border to the Black Sea are booked far in advance, some travelers declaring that the river is the only way to enter Budapest or to see Belgrade. Veteran travelers offer two tips: 1) the Danube is too hot in high summer for long trips by boat, and 2) get detailed information on all the cruise possibilities (Soviet, Romanian, Hungarian, Austrian) before picking one, because some ships are more modern than others.

Sadly, few knowledgeable travel agents will recommend trains any more. The East Orient Express still runs, but slowly and not so comfortably. Only the East Germans and Russians make a big thing of train travel these days; they even have a few luxury cars.

On the road

Does it surprise you to hear that more and more Americans are driving around Eastern Europe today, checking out the back roads? Intourist has a map of the restricted roads open to foreign motorists in the Soviet Union; elsewhere almost everything is open. You'll find relatively few "super highways," but roads are being improved, especially near the coastal resort areas.

Both Hertz and Avis have widespread rental arrangements in most eastern countries, and the national tourist offices also have their own rent-a-car arrangements. At this time only East Germany has no provision for foreigners to rent automobiles, but you can drive one in from West Berlin, Poland or Czechoslovakia.

If you're picking up a new car in Europe and want to drive in the East, there's nothing to stop you. Border controls are thorough but normally not overwhelming. Make sure your car papers are in order and that your insurance covers the country you're entering. (Sometimes it's possible, or even necessary, to buy a limited policy at the frontier.)

Some countries are particularly sensitive about western newspapers; officials may delay you if they think you're carrying too much personal reading matter.

The more venturesome tourist (including the one with less baggage) may want to see more of the country and its people by traveling in local buses. Bus travel is not usually recommended for those in a hurry, but it's still the fastest way to get from Vienna to some of Czechoslovakia's larger cities — and it's cheap.

Budget-minded travelers and those who want to view life from different levels will find a surprisingly extensive network of campsites throughout Eastern Europe. Many are equipped with kitchens and showers.

Languages: no big barrier

It's easier than you think to get along in Eastern Europe, no matter how much trouble you had in Paris with what used to be grade A high school French. The people are friendly, and you'll be surprised at the quality of English spoken by some youths or professional people. Guides and tourist officials usually speak excellent English.

One point: if you want a tour of a museum, make sure it's understood that you want an English guide. Sometimes a guide will show up and assume that everyone in the group is German or French. (If you still have a little high school French or German, give it a try when all else fails. A pair of Oregonians recently used Spanish to buy posters in a Moscow bookstore.)

Shopping made easy

In a bid to get even more tourist dollars, several East European countries have what are commonly called "dollar stores," where tourists or diplomats may buy luxury goods not normally available on the local market or

Outdoor frescoes cover the exterior walls of the Voronet Church in northern Romania's Bukovina region.

Old Town Square *in Cracow, Poland (left) is a favorite gathering place. Ferris wheels, lakes, bandstands, and open-air theaters are all part of Moscow's huge Gorki Park (center). In Hungary's Buda Hills, a favorite viewpoint overlooking Budapest and the Danube is the Fishermen's Bastion (top). Czech dancers relax at a festival (bottom right).*

at much cheaper prices than they sell for locally. The Czechoslovak "Tuzex" stores, popular for records and cut glass objects, and the Soviet "Berioska" shops, which annually sell thousands of fur hats and carved wooden bears, are the most elaborate organizations. But the shopping possibilities aren't limited to the "dollar stores."

Collectors of antiques and icons, the real prizes of East European travel, should get exact and official details on just what may be exported before buying.

Photography restrictions

Some countries have stricter prohibitions than others, but it's well to find out where you stand. In the Soviet Union, for example, you're not allowed to take pictures of bridges because they are considered militarily significant. The U.S. Embassy in Moscow or Intourist, the Soviet travel agency, will give you a list of what is forbidden. Tourist offices and U.S. diplomatic offices in the other countries can also supply details. When in doubt, ask first. And always carry and use your camera openly.

Western films and photo products are difficult, if not impossible, to find in Eastern Europe; Soviet or East German film is usually stocked. Unless you want to experiment, bring enough of your favorite brand. (Regulations limit the number of cameras and rolls of film a tourist can import, just as in western countries, but authorities are usually reasonable.)

Off the beaten track

For an area as large and varied as Eastern Europe, it's difficult in a few lines to suggest where to go. But here are some ideas of places and activities which are not on everyone's itinerary:

Bulgaria. The Rila Monastery, about 75 miles from Sofia, was founded in the 10th century. Set in a pine forest, the buildings remaining today are 19th-century restorations. If you're interested in perfume or marmalade made with roses, try a May or June tour to the source of the raw material in the Valley of the Roses, also a day-trip from Sofia.

Czechoslovakia. Under communist socialized medicine, Czechs can get a doctor's order to restore themselves for a week or two at one of the famous old mineral water resorts, the same spas that used to shelter the crowned heads of Europe and soothe the artistic temperaments of Goethe and Beethoven. If you have a weakness for turn-of-the-century atmosphere, it's still preserved in places like Karlsbad and Marienbad.

East Germany. Old Dresden was heavily damaged in World War II, but the East Germans are proud of what they have done to make it their most popular tourist attraction.

Hungary. Huge Lake Balaton has become such a favorite that private Hungarians are building summer homes there to rent out to foreigners. Touring the lake is a nice day's outing, as is a visit to the Puszta, Hungarian "cowboy" country. Romantics won't be disappointed; gypsy bands serenade everywhere.

Poland. East European veterans are almost unanimous in praise of Cracow. one of the few old towns left untouched by World War II. The center is a gem of Italianate Renaissance architecture. Indeed, the whole city is alive with culture, thanks to thousands of university students in this town associated with Copernicus. For an original treat, try seeing Shakespeare in Polish.

Romania. Don't be put off by the little extra effort it takes to get to the Bukovina region in northeastern Romania, an area distant from Bucharest or the Black Sea resorts. You'll be rewarded by a remarkable attraction: a series of 16th-century monasteries with memorable exterior frescoes.

Soviet Union. That Westerners prefer Leningrad is not surprising, since Peter the Great built it as a western city. But there's new interest in Odessa and other Black Sea resorts, where the Kremlin leaders like to entertain fellow communist officials and foreign notables.

Yugoslavia. Which island can be singled out for praise when the country boasts a thousand, ranging in type from unspoiled to fully developed? The most helpful advice is this: plan early, for the Adriatic coast is no longer "unknown."

Albania. The ninth East European country, listed last because it's still off limits. Albanian authorities at this time still refuse to issue visas to holders of American passports, but politics are shifting fast. This little Adriatic country may open its undeveloped coast to Americans as it has recently to planeloads of Swedes and Britons.

Sports and folklore

Among special activities, you may want to include a hunting or riding trip, or seek out folk festivals. Ask a travel agent or official information office for details.

Hunting. When Neil Armstrong and his Apollo 11 crew visited Yugoslavia, President Tito took them duck shooting. Communist leaders often relax during one of their frequent summit meetings by hunting wild boars or stags. The same activities are open to foreign tourists.

Riding. You can organize a whole vacation or just a day's outing on horseback. If you prefer to be a spectator, ask about the horse shows and jumping competitions. And then there are the race tracks. The "sport of kings" has reached the proletariat, too.

Folklore. Much singing and dancing is performed just for tourists, of course, but even commercial folklore can be fun. Check for dates of religious-oriented festivals where you'll see the most colorful costumes and parades.

TRAVEL INFORMATION ON EASTERN EUROPE

FOR GENERAL INFORMATION	FOR VISA INFORMATION
Bulgarian Tourist Office 50 E. 42nd St., New York, N.Y. 10017	**Bulgarian Legation** 2100 16th St., N.W., Washington, D.C. 20009
Czechoslovak Travel Bureau (Cedok) 10 E. 40th St., New York, N.Y. 10016	**Embassy of Czechoslovakia** 3900 Linnean Ave., N.W., Washington, D.C. 20008
Czechoslovak Airlines—CSA 545 Fifth Ave., New York, N.Y. 10017	
German Democratic Republic Travel Office Alexanderplatz 5, Berlin 102, East Germany (East Germany has no representation in North America.)	East German visas are obtained on arrival on presentation of pre-paid vouchers; there is no East Germany diplomatic representation in North America or Western Europe.
Malév—Hungarian Airlines Rockefeller Center 630 Fifth Ave., Room 2602, New York, N.Y. 10020 (Hungary does not yet have a separate information office.)	**Hungarian Embassy** 2437 15th St., N.W., Washington, D.C. 20009
Polish Travel Office (Orbis) 500 Fifth Ave., New York, N.Y. 10036	**Polish Embassy** 2640 16th St., N.W., Washington, D.C. 20009
Romanian National Tourist Office 500 Fifth Ave., New York, N.Y. 10036	**Romanian Embassy** 1607 23rd St., N.W., Washington, D.C. 20008
Soviet Union Travel Organization (Intourist) 45 E. 49th St., New York, N.Y. 10017	**Embassy of the U.S.S.R.** 1609 Decatur St., N.W., Washington, D.C. 20011
Aeroflot Soviet Airlines 545 Fifth Ave., New York, N.Y. 10017	
Yugoslav National Tourist Office 630 Fifth Ave., New York, N.Y. 10020	**Yugoslav Embassy** 2410 California Ave., N.W., Washington, D.C. 20008

INDEX

PHOTOGRAPHERS

Austrian National Tourist Office: pages 76, 77, 78, 79, 80, 81, 82, 83. **Belgian Tourist Office:** pages 60, 61 (bottom left), 62. **Mimi Brandes:** page 84. **British Tourist Authority:** pages 8, 9 (top left, bottom, right), 12, 13, 14, 16, 17 (left, top right, bottom right), 19, 20, 21, 23, 24. **Bulgarian Tourist Office:** page 154 (top center). **Casa de Portugal:** page 129 (left). **Glenn Christiansen:** pages 153 (center), 156 (center). **Kenneth Cooperrider:** page 73 (right). **Czechoslovak Travel Bureau:** page 156 (bottom right). **Danish National Tourist Office:** pages 141 (left, bottom center), 142, 143, 144, 145 (top, bottom left, center), 147 (bottom left). **Nancy Davidson:** pages 27 (top left), 28, 29. **Richard Dawson:** pages 90 (center), 116, 117, 145 (right). **Jerry DiVecchio:** page 150. **Joan Perry Dutton:** page 121 (left). **Finnish National Tourist Office:** pages 141 (top), 148, 149. **Richard Fish:** pages 11 (bottom right), 35 (right), 47 (left), 99 (center). **Cornelia Fogle:** back cover (center), pages 10, 11 (left, top), 15, 18, 22 (center, right), 34, 35 (left, top center, bottom center), 37 (left), 38 (left, right), 39, 46, 47 (top, center, right), 53 (right), 66, 67 (top, bottom left, right) 70, 89 (left, right), 93 (top left), 126 (center, right), 132, 156 (top right). **French Government Tourist Office:** front cover, pages 36, 37 (right), 40, 41, 43, 44. **German National Tourist Office:** back cover (top), pages 2, 64, 65, 67 (center), 71 (left, right), 74. **Norman Gordon:** pages 102, 103 (left), 112, 113 (left). **Greek National Tourist Organization:** pages 110, 111 (top, right, bottom left), 113 (right). **Jay Hoops Studios:** page 111 (center). **Irish Tourist Board:** pages 26, 27 (bottom left, center, right), 30, 31, 90 (right). **Italian Government Travel Office:** 96, 97, 98, 99 (top, bottom left, right), 100, 101, 103 (right), 104, 105, 106, 107, 108. **Dorothy Krell:** page 127. **Roy Krell:** pages 52, 72, 73 (left), 124, 128, 129 (top center, bottom center, right), 130. **Martin Litton:** pages 9 (top center), 53 (left), 68, 69, 71 (center), 90 (left). **Luxembourg Tourist Office:** pages 58, 59. **Proctor Mellquist:** pages 153 (left), 154 (left, bottom center). **Charles Mohler:** pages 17 (center), 42. **Josef Muench:** page 48. **Netherlands National Tourist Office:** back cover (bottom), pages 6, 50, 51, 53 (center), 54, 55, 56, 57. **Norwegian National Tourist Office:** pages 133, 134, 135, 136, 141 (right), 147 (right). **Lou Siebert Pappas:** pages 22 (left), 38 (center). **Polish Travel Office:** pages 153 (right), 156 (left). **Romanian National Tourist Office:** pages 126 (left), 155. **Cynthia Scheer:** page 45. **Alastair Simpson:** page 32. **Mary Benton Smith:** page 61 (top, right). **Soviet Union Travel Organization:** page 152. **Spanish National Tourist Office:** 119, 120, 121 (right), 122, 123, 125. **Rick Sullivan:** page 114. **Swedish National Tourist Office:** pages 137, 138, 139, 140, 147 (top). **Swiss National Tourist Office:** pages 7, 86, 87, 88, 89 (center), 91, 92, 93 (center, right, bottom), 94. **Yugoslav National Tourist Office:** page 154 (left).